FALL OUT

WORLD WAR II AND
THE SHAPING OF POSTWAR EUROPE

BY THE SAME AUTHOR

Nuremberg: The Facts, the Law and the Consequences
Survey of International Affairs 1947–48
Survey of International Affairs 1949–50
Survey of International Affairs 1951
Survey of International Affairs 1952
Survey of International Affairs 1953
Middle East Crisis (with Guy Wint)
South Africa and World Opinion
World Order and New States
Suez: Ten Years After (with Anthony Moncrieff)
World Politics since 1945 (7th Edition, 1996)
Total War (with Guy Wint and John Pritchard)
The British Experience 1945–75
Freedom to Publish (with Ann Bristow)
Top Secret Ultra
Independent Africa and the World
A Time for Peace
Who's Who in the Bible
Resilient Europe: A Study of the Years 1870–2000
Threading My Way (Memoirs)

FALL OUT

World War II and the Shaping of Postwar Europe

Peter Calvocoressi

LONGMAN
London and New York

Addison Wesley Longman Limited
Edinburgh Gate
Harlow
Essex   CM20 2JE
United Kingdom
and Associated Companies throughout the world

Published in the United States of America
by Addison Wesley Longman Inc., New York

First published 1997

ISBN   0 582 30908 5   CSD
       0 582 30907 7   PPR

British Library Cataloguing-in-Publication Data

A catalogue record for this book is available from the British Library

Library of Congress Cataloging-in-Publication Data

A catalog entry for this book is available from the Library of Congress

Set by 35 in 11/12 pt Baskerville
Produced by Longman Singapore Publishers (Pte) Ltd.
Printed in Singapore

CONTENTS

INTRODUCTION

In this book I address the impact of World War II on the never-ending process of the shaping of Europe. More precisely, I address those issues of World War II which, besides being still contentious, bear particularly on postwar Europe, and I do so in a series of essays which are interlocking reflections on these issues.

Was World War II a war against Germany or a war against fascism? Did it, from either cause, have to be fought to a finish with the unconditional surrender of Germany as a necessary objective and the postwar pattern of Europe – including the Cold War – as a necessary sequel? Has it settled, or at least altered, the German Question which has plagued Europe for over a century and more and has devastated large parts of it? Has the mind of Germany been changed? Where stands or lurks fascism now? These questions were not new, nor were they disposed of by the war, but the war is the largest single item in their current manifestation.

Wars are most simply defined in antagonistic terms. They are against somebody or something. The somebody is characteristically a state, the something a complex of ideas, secular or religious. In modern times when it has become necessary to enlist the energies and risk the lives of very large numbers of people, there is a growing need to give wars a more positive and more uplifting justification than bare antagonism: to define them as being for something rather than against somebody. War aims have come to include the attempt to put an end to war or at least curtail its frequency or – more vaguely and more grandly – to strangle wickedness. The paradox of a war to end war is not as silly as it sounds, for undoubtedly war concentrates the mind wonderfully, and

1

although the principal target of this concentration is victory, enduring peace is another. Even in the press of war there is room for thinking about a less violent and anarchic political order, and the more horrible the war the more radical the thinking is likely to become.

The search for alternatives to war as a means of settling disputes or disposing of villains has been a specially European endeavour. Its central feature has been law – the use of law as a preventive or antidote by, first, clarifying international law regarding war, violent conflict and gross inhumanity and, secondly, applying the law to states and to their rulers. There are two strands to this endeavour. Both are addressed in this book.

The first is juridical. It led after World War II to the Nuremberg and other trials for war crimes and other international misdemeanours. These trials sought to apply the laws of war to individuals and, further, to examine the law where it ought to be examined, that is to say, before a competent tribunal. They also demonstrated, if only coincidentally, that legal action was largely the outcome of nonlegal revulsion against such enormities as the indiscriminate bombing of civilians and their homes and the slaughter by Germans of Jews, Slavs and other categories of human being merely for being what they were. The impulse was as much moral as legal. Less obvious at the time, but no less crucial, was the role of war itself, for war and total defeat provided – as nothing else could provide – the opportunity for the considerable steps taken at Nuremberg in probing and applying the law. War and victory were preconditions for the trials. But these preconditions are rare and in themselves highly undesirable, so that hopes of amplifying and continuing to apply what was pioneered at Nuremberg have been dimmed. Since Nuremberg there have been similar crimes galore but no similar trials. The law was asserted but in a context which has not been replicated. The establishment by the United Nations of special tribunals to examine allegations of crimes in Bosnia and Rwanda may further the rule of law in this field or expose the frustrating limitations of such ventures.

The second strand in Europe's search for a more peaceful future is political. Since the seventeenth century, to go back no further, western Europe has been an agglomeration of independent secular states with a legal doctrine of sovereignty to match this pre-eminent political fact. Power has been distributed among states of varying weight and increasing number. This situation automatically generated hostility among the states and in order to moderate or control this latent anarchy statesmen developed the notion of balancing power in the hope that the permutations of political alliances would inhibit wars. But a balance of power was more a principle than a fact, for there is no point of balance where a states system may become reliably fixed, and the operators of the system used its adaptability as much to establish dominance as to create equilibrium. In practice, moreover, it was close to impossible for any one state to operate a policy of balance with the fallible tools at its command for measuring the power of other states. The system may have inhibited some wars which never took place but it repeatedly and logically led to numerous wars, culminating in the calamitous outbreaks of destruction of the present century. As a means for reducing war in a states system the balance of power was a broken reed. It may be argued that the experiences of the twentieth century have done enough to blunt Europe's appetite for war, but the same could have been said of the Wars of Religion of the seventeenth century which, like the wars of our own time, stimulated the search for a better system but did not find one. The European wars of the twentieth century rubbed in the lesson that the state itself is a potent source of war. But for Europeans the subordination of the state is as radical a shift in the organisation of power and the demarcation of loyalties as anything attempted in 500 years of European history.

The Cold War which quickly followed World War II smothered debate about re-ordering Europe's political constitution. A different debate supervened. In European terms the Cold War was a violent rift with European tradition because it emphasised ideological rather than territorial issues. It was about beliefs or pretended beliefs, not states or their borders. Nor was it about Europe, although it began there. And it exposed the relegation of Europeans from world-beaters while leaving them more than ever dependent on extra-European materials, finance and links. But the Cold

War ended, as its saner observers always maintained that it would, and therewith the question of Europe returned to the top of Europe's agenda. It did so in terms which had been mooted during World War II and tentatively espoused during the Cold War. Both these conflicts radicalised political trends already in the wind and emboldened the proponents of a unification which challenged long-established facts, settled ideas, entrenched loyalties and vested interests. If to many Europeans the debasement of the sovereign state is as disturbing as the vision – or nightmare – of Europe as an element in an American-Soviet gigantomachia, yet a union in some form or other could solve the German Question (no other solution presented itself); might reduce war in Europe more effectively than balance of power *ad hoc*-ery and more effectively than the Covenant of the League or the UN Charter; and could create a European force capable of playing the substantially independent role in world affairs no longer attainable by Europe's separate states. For political debate of this nature Europeans have had a taste for two and a half millennia.

Europe has two special and inalienable advantages. First, it has a degree of cultural homogeneity. This is a *sine qua non* of effective cooperation: it is what the UN, for example, does not have. Secondly, Europe is small. Whether you look at a map or at the categorisation imposed upon the world by common continental terminology, Europe has definition without extension. This is another gift, for in spite of the marvels of communications technology from the aeroplane to the fax machine and extraterrestrial intercourse, physical distance still works powerfully on the minds of men and conditions such humdrum activities as administration. After World War I H.G. Wells wrote of 'the great effort to reconstruct the world'. That has proved too utopian a task for practical politicians and a happy hunting ground for cynics. World War II raised the more manageable prospect of refashioning Europe and that is perhaps the most signal legacy of the war's uncompromising defeat of Germany. This book ends with a survey of the ensuing fifty years when radical changes in world power set powerful new conditions for debate over Europe's affairs: conditions which look rather different at the end of the half century from the assumptions commonly made at its beginning.

INTRODUCTION

All the essays in this book are published here for the first time except the last, which originated, with slight differences, as an Occasional Paper of the David Davies Memorial Institute of International Studies.

PETER CALVOCORESSI
Bath, November 1996

Chapter 1

UNCONDITIONAL SURRENDER

I

In January 1943 at Casablanca in Morocco Roosevelt and Churchill agreed and announced that their countries would not negotiate the end of the war with the Axis Powers on any terms whatever. They would accept only unconditional surrender, although they did not use that phrase. The declaration, which was carried into effect when Germany capitulated on 8 May 1945, has been much criticised, mainly on the grounds that it prolonged the war.

The month of January 1943 has commonly been identified as the turning point in the war. It did not seem so at the time. On the contrary, the prevailing mood was uncertainty. There were on the one hand positive achievements, but there were also perplexity and disagreement about what to do next and shortages of equipment. The campaigns in Africa – in Libya and North West Africa – were being wound up, but they were peripheral to the main theatre and they were as yet disappointingly unfinished. The Americans had arrived in force, but not on the European continent. The Mediterranean had been reconquered and the Battle of the Atlantic had taken a turn for the better, but the war in the air between the British and American bombers and the German fighter defences was undecided. So was the war on the eastern front about which the western allies knew less than they would have liked to know. In 1941 the Germans had failed to take Moscow or Leningrad and they failed again in 1942 when they switched their main effort towards the Caucasus. While Roosevelt and Churchill were conferring at Casablanca, the German armies and air forces were on the verge of their huge defeat at Stalingrad and, again in retrospect, it is plausible to treat that battle as Hitler's irreversible defeat in the east.[1] But Germany's military output was rising, its morale seemed undented, its secret weapons were an unknown quantity and – for the very few in the big secret – its known attempt to produce a nuclear bomb could not be written off as the failure which later it turned out to be.

There was, therefore, as much fog as jubilation at Casablanca in January 1943 and the demand for unconditional surrender was one of the things – one of the few concrete things – which emerged from the fog. The demand was directed against Italy as well as Germany. The Italian aspect was little, if at all, considered. In Roosevelt's eyes and Churchill's the Italians were already beaten. Italy was included in the declaration more because it would have seemed odd to leave it out than for any other reason, and the war with Italy was brought to an end by two armistice agreements in November 1943, less than a year after the Casablanca conference. The negotiations were with the fascist government minus Mussolini who had been dismissed by the king in July and imprisoned (he was rescued by the Germans in September). These negotiations were secret and muddled. They took the Italians out of the war but not the Germans out of Italy, where the war went on until the general capitulation twenty months later. Neither in the case of Italy nor in that of Japan did the demand for unconditional surrender inhibit making peace on other terms when it seemed expedient to do so.[2]

1. If it was not, then the Kursk battles in 1943 were. From the one point or the other Hitler had lost control of the war in the east. His strategies thereafter served only to make that defeat total and extravagant. The retrospective question is: would the German invasion of the Soviet Union in 1941 have had a different outcome if the Americans had not been brought into the war by Hitler in December of that year? In the light of Hitler's failures before Moscow and Leningrad in 1941, capped by his failures in 1942, it is difficult to suppose so. All these things happened before the Americans arrived in Africa. British and American help to Stalin in the intervening period was valuable but marginal.
2. The United States and Britain demanded the unconditional surrender of Japan – until almost the end of the war. Their last demand, in August 1945, was modified by demanding only the surrender of Japan's armed

7

The Casablanca declaration was part gesture, part policy. It was one of those things which seem less significant at the time than they do later – in which respect it was the opposite of another piece of conference-inspired verbiage, the Atlantic Charter, which seemed more significant at its birth than it did later. The Casablanca conference was both a celebration and a foretaste of uneasiness to come. The allied leaders had more possibilities than instruments to fulfil them (they were particularly short of the landing craft essential for returning to the European continent and for operations elsewhere). They were uneasily aware that only the Russians were fighting on the European mainland and they were at least subliminally anxious to do, or at any rate say, something pleasing to them. If Stalin feared that his allies might make a separate peace and leave him in the lurch, the reverse was also true. The Casablanca declaration was beamed at Moscow as much as Germany. Its uncompromising tone may also have been influenced by the growing awareness during 1942 of the atrocities perpetrated by Germans in Europe, but it is impossible to weigh this factor beyond saying that it made a subordinate contribution.

The origins of the declaration are not straightforward. Its authors seem to have become uneasy about it soon after they issued it, for the accounts which they gave are untrue. Roosevelt maintained that it was a subsidiary, almost accidental issue and Churchill gave the impression that he complied because he was taken by surprise and could see no good reason for not complying. In fact, however, some such declaration had been under debate in Washington for nearly a year, had been submitted by Roosevelt to Churchill five months before Casablanca with a strong request for its endorsement and had been considered by the British cabinet. Churchill himself had reservations about applying it to Italy,

---

forces, implying the reprieve of Japan's sacred monarchy. This was one factor in the Japanese capitulation. There were others: the nuclear devastation of Hiroshima and Nagasaki, and Japan's failure to get Stalin to desert his allies and agree not to invade Japan. The Japanese government, as the Americans knew from deciphering their diplomatic traffic, was unwilling to surrender but not unanimously or irreversibly. Even after Nagasaki the Japanese cabinet was divided and indecisive. The decision to surrender was taken by the emperor and conveyed by him to cabinet and people.

but did not press them and raised no more than minor verbal points. The phrase 'unconditional surrender' rang a bell with Americans who were familiar with General Ulysees S. Grant's famous and successful challenge to General Robert E. Lee which ended the American Civil War. The Union had offered the Confederacy terms which the Confederate President Jefferson Davis rejected because they did not give the South independence. The war went on, but was soon brought to an end by military necessity which made Grant's demand for unconditional surrender unrefusable. This outcome gave the victorious North a free hand – and there is nothing more satisfying than a free hand. The Civil War did much to implant in the American mind a view of war as a win-or-lose activity. This was not the European tradition, in which wars have been habitually ended by treaties and congresses whose names are as well known as the battles which preceded them and whose main purpose has been to negotiate or ratify terms.

Another historical memory came from the way World War I ended. Although the German armies were defeated in France in 1918, legend subsequently denied this verdict, asserting that the German surrender had been necessitated by a collapse of civilian morale. The inference that Germany had all but beaten the western allies as well as the Russians strengthened those who looked to a second round of military aggression to reverse defeat and retrieve national honour. In fact, Germany failed only narrowly to score a decisive victory in 1918, but not on account of a stab in the back by spineless civilians. In the second war there was an undercurrent of feeling that a victory this time must be unambiguous and likewise unconditional in the sense that there must be nothing like Woodrow Wilson's Fourteen Points which could be used to argue that the losers had agreed to end hostilities on terms offered and then broken by the victors.

But more potent than past memories were present realities and among them was the need to sustain the alliance with the Soviet Union. In spite of the vaunted and feared prowess of the Luftwaffe, Hitler's greatest strength was in his armies and they were in Russia. Had they not been on the eastern front they would be on the western where they would have made an Anglo-American invasion of the continent all but impossible. By invading the Soviet Union Hitler had denuded his western front and by resisting the German invasion Stalin had kept it denuded. But Stalin had been suspicious of the west for a lifetime and he made none of the hard distinctions which Roosevelt and Churchill made between Anglo-American democrats and German Nazis: for Stalin they were all anti-communists. The mission of the deputy Führer Rudolf Hess to Britain and Anglo-American prevarications over the timing of a second front against Hitler in France fuelled these suspicions, and Stalin was fearful that after their victories in Africa the western allies would consider a separate peace with Germany which would leave the Soviet Union not merely in the cold but in the direst peril. The western allies had similar suspicions – they remembered the Soviet deal with Hitler as recently as 1939 – and they had too a similar need for the alliance if they wished to prosecute the war by an invasion of France sooner or later.[3] The Casablanca declaration was designed to allay Russian fears of a separate Western–German peace and so diminish the risks of a separate Soviet–German peace. It was far from certain in the winter of 1942–43 that Stalin would or could fight to the bitter end. The great tank battles of 1943, which proved the point, were still to come and at Casablanca the survival of the Soviet Union and its will to continue fighting were a more pressing problem than visions of what the Russians might do in eastern and central Europe if ever they got there.

The western allies attached considerable importance to psychological warfare or, in a word, morale. They found it difficult to believe that the odious Nazi regime could be broadly or deeply popular and they proposed to assail this supposedly weak point by the mass bombing of homes and workplaces. They were much less mindful of minority groups of anti-Nazi Germans and they have in retrospect been

---

3. Roosevelt developed a similar view of the need for Russian help against Japan, but the two cases were different in that his wooing of Stalin to join the war against Japan was an unnecessary manoeuvre which benefited the Soviet Union without commensurate benefit to the United States. It created the one major postwar issue which was still unsettled half a century later: the Russo-Japanese dispute over the Kurile Islands. Neither Gorbachev nor Yeltsin was able to settle this dispute and Japan refused to join international schemes for economic aid for post-communist Russia.

accused not only of undervaluing these groups but of undermining them by, among other mistakes, their demand for unconditional surrender which could leave the German populace worse off in defeat than in the last ditch with Hitler and his regime.

Many Germans hated Hitler and some conspired against him. Others were tempted to conspire but did not. Between Nazis and anti-Nazis was a mass of non-Nazis who were neither expected to conspire nor in a position to do so. There were potent forces at work on both sides. The Gestapo was well informed about grumblers and plotters and the penalties were ferocious. The authorities had no inhibitions about the use of the most devilish tortures and conspirators were well aware of the terrible consequences of being detected or merely suspected. On the other hand there was a variety of reasons for opposition to Hitler. Before the war and in its early stages these reasons were diverse and ill-coordinated. In the army there was universal approval of rearmament, but enough resentment, professional and snobbish, against Hitler's intrusion into its affairs to cause him in 1938 to reshuffle the top positions – evidence of his sensitiveness to military opinion, but also of his ability to control it without alienating the army as a whole. Officers wanted the best equipment and more of it, but they were not so united in their readiness to go to war and certainly not to go to war with too many enemies at once or with Hitler himself as commander-in-chief. Christians were appalled by his attacks on their churches, his indifference to their beliefs and his extreme disdain of their standards of behaviour, but they were divided between outright revulsion and politic conciliation, frequently too ready to discern non-existent silver linings to black clouds. Prominent Protestants such as Bishop Wurm of Würzburg might be admired as valiant martyrs and upholders of Christian values but they could also be criticised for making things worse by sticking their necks out. Roman Catholics, in Germany and in the Vatican, could argue for caution and humility in the face of evil, for striking a bargain with the Devil who, in the shape of Hitler, was a fervent anti-communist and the readier to conclude a treaty with the Vatican (as Mussolini had done in 1929) because he felt free to interpret it any way he chose once he had signed it. Liberals and democrats, whether Christian or not, anathematised

11

Nazism, while of socialists and Jews, so far as they were left alive, it is unnecessary to speak: their hatred was with good cause axiomatic. The opposition included patricians with famous names from Kleist to Bismarck; civil and military public servants, notably Karl Goerdeler, former mayor of Leipzig, and Field Marshal Ludwig Beck, former chief of staff of the army; influential persons still in government service such as Admiral Wilhelm Canaris, chief of military intelligence (the Abwehr) and ambassador Ulrich von Hassell; Christians such as Helmuth von Moltke, Peter Yorck von Wartenburg and Adam von Trott zu Solz; leaders of banned left-wing parties and workers' unions. These various groups came increasingly, if slowly, together with one another, but were mostly without power.[4]

Before war came in 1939, what anti-Nazi Germans wanted of the outside world, pre-eminently Britain, was precise statements and policies which would check Hitler, cause him to lose face and so open the way for some action leading to a change of government in Berlin. The aim – the elimination of Hitler – was clear but the means and the sequel were not. Even the future role of a Nazi Party without Hitler was unclear, for the disappearance of Hitler would not necessarily or even probably cause the disappearance of his party, which was the largest in the Reichstag and undoubtedly popular with the public.[5] But the weaknesses of the opposition were not the principal causes of its failure to attract foreign sympathy and support. Its aims were the reverse of Chamberlain's. The British prime minister was intent not on unseating Hitler but on doing a deal with him which would prevent war: peace, for Chamberlain and his like, was paramount. The Munich conference of 1938 clearly demonstrated Britain's reliance on Hitler as a principal in a strategy for peace. The

---

4. *Withstanding Hitler* by Michael Balfour (London, 1988) is the most penetrating account in English of the fearful moral and practical problems faced by Hitler's German enemies. It contains invaluable sketches of the backgrounds, beliefs and activities of thirty of them.
5. Anybody who went to Germany in the 1930s, as I did for several years running, could see that Hitler was widely regarded not as a monster but as a redeemer who had restored German self-esteem and raised the standard of living. This veneration was not easily killed. Even the defeats in the east from the surrender at Stalingrad onwards were blamed on Hitler's generals rather than on him.

German plotters were greatly dispirited by Munich, but they renewed their efforts after the conference, largely because there was nothing else to be done.

Once war had begun, the plotters' aims inevitably changed. They regarded the war as a disastrous mistake and wanted to end what they had not been able to prevent, but plotting in wartime was much more problematical than plotting in peacetime, partly because in a country at war it was treason and partly because the plotters, particularly army officers, were scattered abroad: most of the German army spent most of the war outside Germany. From 1941 a new element was introduced by Hitler's attack on the Soviet Union, which officers as well as others regarded as military madness and, from about 1943, as opening the door to far-flung communist victories. They were deeply anti-communist, whether as members of privileged castes or as Christians. They made the mistake of supposing the western allies to be equally anti-communist and willing to end the war in order to stem the Red Peril. They therefore sought a negotiated peace and tried to discover on what terms and conditions the western allies would negotiate; they did not envisage – or very few envisaged – negotiations with the Soviet Union. German church leaders who went to Stockholm in May 1942 to meet Dr George Bell, bishop of Chichester, were ready to pledge a new German government to make reparation to Poland and Czechoslovakia for war damage (but were less precise about postwar frontiers) and to compensate Jews for what had been done to them and their property in Germany. They got little in return apart from a speech by the bishop in the House of Lords urging the government to insist that Britain was making war only on Nazism. As the military situation in the east deteriorated and a *putsch*, with or without foreign encouragement, became increasingly unlikely, they turned in despair, and with considerable moral misgivings and division among themselves, to the last resort of assassinating Hitler. Over the last two years of war a dozen plots were concocted, all of them unsuccessful for reasons which had nothing to do with the Casablanca declaration.

But getting rid of Hitler was not a sufficient aim. It needed to be preceded and accompanied by the coordination and swift implementation of a post-Nazi regime. And it had to be done by the military, for although the assassin's trigger might be pulled by anybody, only powerful and pre-arranged support could ensure the seizure of power by anti-Nazi forces upon the fall of the dictator. But army officers were hard to persuade. Apart from their oath of loyalty, which was to some extent an excuse for inaction, they often spoke bitterly or viciously against Hitler in private but found reasons for doing nothing more effective to stop the disasters which they blamed on him. The much-respected elder Field Marshal Gerd von Rundstedt was one of these and the outstandingly successful Field Marshal Eric von Manstein was another. The famous Panzer General Heinz Guderian undertook to beard Hitler about his strategies, but when face to face with the Führer did precisely the opposite. The most effective of the wartime chiefs of staff of the army, General Franz Halder, blew evasively hot and cold; his superior, Field Marshal Walther von Brauchitsch, only cold. The conspirators' most likely catch, Field Marshal Gunther von Kluge, always backed away from decisive action at the critical moment. Many were tested but few were reliable, and with the passage of time leaks to the Gestapo multiplied and the chances of concerted action diminished. In March 1943 an attempt to kill Hitler by blowing up the aircraft in which he was returning from Smolensk on the eastern front to his HQ at Rastenburg in East Prussia failed: the explosives in two bottles of brandy did not go off. But the failure was not merely technical. The plan's principal authors, the intrepid Colonel Henning von Tresckow and the peacetime lawyer Fabian von Schlabrendorff, concluded that the second essential – efficient coordination of immediate action in Berlin and elsewhere – had been inadequately prepared. By 1944 the game was becoming even more dangerous and urgent. Himmler was increasingly well informed; the conspirators' main coordinator in Berlin, General Hans Oster, was removed from his post, presumably at the instigation of the Gestapo; and military collapse in the east came clearly nearer. Tresckow found a singularly brave and well-connected ally in Count Claus von Stauffenberg, a South German aristocrat who, after two aborted attempts, placed two powerful bombs a few yards from Hitler on 20 July 1944. The plan was bungled and the outcome a disaster from which the opposition never recovered. Hitler was blown through a window but escaped death or serious injury and the plan of action in Berlin was half implemented and then completely overwhelmed. A few, including Tresckow, committed suicide. Many were tortured for months and executed.

In one obvious sense the opposition was a total failure. It failed to kill Hitler and had no impact on the course or length of the war. But it was far from a failure in the longer term. The men and women who immersed themselves in these fearsome activities salvaged much from the degrading and calamitous years 1933–45 and posterity has not denied them their due for their courage and their steadfastness in the face of unimagined peril and evil. What was denied by contemporaries and by posterity is effectiveness. Judgement is in the nature of things difficult, but there is something distasteful and disconcerting about the ease with which these serious and brave persons were dismissed by the western allies as insignificant or incompetent or unrepresentative or merely self-interested. Some of them were some of these things some of the time: for example, some were strangely careless about allowing the Gestapo to know who they were and what they were doing, while others were stirred to thoughts of action against Hitler only when his survival threatened theirs. Some of them believed that the allied demand for unconditional surrender made their task significantly harder. Adam von Trott, for example, asked how any group of Germans could hope to win support for an anti-Hitler coup so long as Germany's enemies continued to wage war *a outrance*. The British were sceptical, believing them doomed to ineffectiveness whether or not they got expressions of goodwill from outside Germany or promises about the postwar treatment of Germany. The allies could not deliver and were not asked to deliver material aid of the kind that they were delivering to resistance movements in German-occupied Europe: the German opposition was not a resistance movement of this kind and could not conceivably become one. The allies could make statements about distinguishing the German people from Nazi criminals and had done so from the outset of the war, but they doubted whether such statements did anything to hamper the German war effort or sap the German will to resist. It takes a great deal of fantasy to suppose that the cynics were wrong.

In Britain and America, the two belligerents whose leaders made the Casablanca declaration, the distinction between Germans and Nazis was explicit from the beginning of the war to its end, frequently repeated and virtually unquestioned. Churchill consistently referred to the enemy as Nazis, not Germans. Primitive nationalism was remarkable by its absence. (In Britain it was more pronounced against Helmuth Kohl's government than Hitler's.) The distinction was not so clearly drawn in continental Europe, but no continental country had a voice at Casablanca or counted for much in allied counsels between Casablanca and the end of the war. The conditions ruled out by the declaration were never clearly specified, but they may be broadly identified as undertakings of two kinds: territorial terms and other retributive or punitive impositions, mainly economic. Hitler had made a number of conquests which Germans of all kinds would be loathe to renounce, particularly the forcible incorporation of Austria into the German Reich and the annexation of Danzig and its hinterland, perhaps too the Sudetenland. The Casablanca declaration demanded surrender on the basis that all German conquests would be considered and settled by the victors alone without prior engagements before the war ended and, implicitly, without consultation with a new German government after the war. It is hard to see how, from 1943 onward, this stance could be judged unreasonable or as prolonging the war. Other conditions might include limitations on the size of the German armed forces, but the principal concern of Germans looking into the future was economic: restrictions on German industry and punitive reparations. In the United States, but not to any significant extent in Britain, there was a body of opinion which, with a mixture of (ill-considered) *Realpolitik* and vindictiveness, wished to cripple Germany economically as many in France had wished to do after World War I. This line of thought produced the Morgenthau Plan (Henry Morgenthau was Roosevelt's secretary of the treasury) for the partition, deindustrialisation and pastoralisation of Germany which was presented to the Quebec conference in September 1944 and there endorsed by Roosevelt and Churchill. It was quickly jettisoned. The State Department and the Foreign Office – and hopeful British exporters – thought it insane and European producers, had they been consulted, would have been even more censorious. The damage, if any, was short-lived.

The Casablanca declaration, and *per contra* any reassurances about the future treatment of a defeated Germany which allied leaders might have given but did not, could have affected the anti-Nazi silent mass, one way or the other, more or less. The crucial question, however, is whether a different allied policy would have strengthened the chances of a *putsch*: which means whether it would have stiffened senior army waverers like von Kluge. The question is, of course, unanswerable, but scepticism is inescapable. Von Kluge and his like were what they were and what they were was not the work of the Casablanca declaration. They were convinced that the war was lost and they were deeply concerned about the postwar fortunes of Germany at the hands of victorious enemies, but far and away their principal concern was to break the Grand Alliance, make peace in the west without making peace in the east and – at some time, sooner or later – to secure a reversal of alliances which would inaugurate a new war to destroy the Soviet Union and communism. This grand aim was entirely unreal, and if *per impossibile* the western allies had been minded to entertain it they would not have been deterred by the Casablanca or any other declaration. Churchill was famously hostile to communism and much worried about the expansion of Soviet power into the heart of Europe, but he was not going to break faith with Stalin, while Roosevelt was determined to carry the American-Soviet alliance over into peacetime and sufficiently hopeful to make it the keystone of his world-view. Hitler's own German enemies wanted a sign, but the sign sought by the generals and field marshals with the power to make a coup was a sign which no properly informed person could conceivably have expected.

As the war's end approached, military leaders such as von Kluge – and the Reichsführer SS Heinrich Himmler who was in command of armies on the eastern front at this stage – were willing to talk about surrender, but not unconditional surrender and not surrender to the Russians as well as the western allies. These men had the power to shorten the war but they wanted to use their power to shorten half the war, not the whole of it, and in spite of the sacrifices involved in fighting on (postwar consequences as well as wartime sacrifices) it would have been impossibly dishonourable for Roosevelt or Churchill to accept or even to consider an armistice on these terms. The obstacle was not unconditional surrender; it was the particular conditions attached to the surrender envisaged by Hitler's German adversaries. The war ran its full course to unconditional surrender because the combatants were never within sight of any other way to end it, and this conclusion was due above all to the east/west alliance without which the war might have ended with a German victory or a stalemate and a negotiated compromise. Either of these outcomes would, to say the least, have been unhappy – not least for Germany.

. . .

II

The allied demand for unconditional surrender enunciated at Casablanca had a positive ring, but it concealed a negative irresolution. It was addressed to Germans at large and to the Soviet government, i.e. Stalin, in particular. On the course of events in Germany it had imperceptible or no effect, on Stalin perhaps some effect, but one which cannot be calculated; its importance is easily exaggerated. At that date the war was for the Americans a little over a year old, for the British over three years old and past its midpoint; but it had another two and a quarter years to run. The failure of Hitler's plan to destroy the Soviet Union in a matter of months was becoming apparent even if the final outcome on the eastern fronts was not. The odds on victory over Germany were good. The problems of a postwar settlement were therefore seeping onto the agenda.

Germany's enemies had to make up their minds what they wanted of this settlement and it went without saying that the possible programmes were equal to the number of Germany's principal enemies. In the event there was no formal treaty of peace with Germany because the victors disagreed about its terms and ended the war in positions from which no one of them could impose its will on the others. This stalemate was one of the outstanding consequences of World War II. It arose from the manner of the defeat of the German armies in the fighting on the eastern front and from the timing of the resumption of the fighting in France.

The western allies wanted Stalin to beat Hitler, but they were nonplussed by the scale of Stalin's victories and their political implications, for Stalin conquered not only the German armies but the whole of eastern and central Europe excepting only countries with Mediterranean or Adriatic coastlines – Greece, Yugoslavia, Albania. In this large area the postwar settlement was not about German expansion but Soviet expansion and with the Soviet armies in sole possession the western allies were reduced to argument unsupported by power. The force of their arguments was conditioned by the distribution of military power at the approach of the German defeat and this pattern was in turn conditioned by the timing of the invasion of France.

It has been argued, notably by John Grigg in his book *1943: The Victory That Never Was*[6] (and of course by Stalin), that the western allies could and should have opened a second front against Germany at least a year earlier than they did. The consequences, had they done so successfully, would have been momentous and ironically Stalin, who was bitterly critical of his allies' delays, would have been the principal loser if they had felt able to start on their way into Germany in 1943 when Stalin was embroiled in the tremendous battles around Kursk thousands of miles away.[7] In all probability the war would have been shorter, fewer people – civilians as well as men and women in the armed services – would have been killed, less damage would have been inflicted on homes and workplaces, less wealth would have been blown away and the war would have ended without the Russians in occupation of Prague, Vienna and Berlin. The postwar history of Britain would have been less burdensome and less dependent. Neither the Iron Curtain nor the

6. John Grigg, *1943: The Victory That Never Was* (New York, 1982).
7. The Battle of Kursk made evident the defeat of the Germans by the Soviet armies. It lasted from the first week of July 1943 to the middle of August. The Kursk salient stretched 80 miles from north to south and over 100 miles westward. It was potentially either a springboard for a Soviet offensive or an opportunity for a German pincer movement to entrap the five Soviet armies within it. The battle was launched, after numerous delays, by the Germans towards the nodal city of Kursk in the middle of the salient. It quickly failed on both the salient's flanks. Soviet offensives towards Orel to the north and Kharkov to the south were then successful. Four million men fought and 6,000 tanks and 12,000 aircraft, the Germans being outnumbered in both these arms. The simultaneous allied landings in Sicily and threat to Italy had some impact, either by forcing Hitler to withdraw forces from his eastern front or by giving him a pretext to scale down a lost battle. After Kursk the question was not who might win in the east but how quickly the Russians would get where.

Cold War would have been what they were, although they probably would have come about in some other form. Had all these ifs and buts been present to the minds of statesmen and strategists, would they have thrown some of their caution to the breezes and attempted an invasion in 1943? It is probably just as well that they did not. John Grigg's critique is mainly a polemic against the invasion of Sicily and the Italian peninsula in 1943 which, he argues, should have been undertaken either sooner or not at all. He maintains that the refusal to invade northern France in 1943 was due to misconceived strategy together with a lack not of resources but of will – notably among the British who succeeded in dissuading the Americans from a quick invasion which in British eyes was not merely too risky, but positively impracticable.

There were a number of plans. *Sledgehammer* was a plan to invade in 1942. When Molotov visited Washington that year Roosevelt gave him the impression that an invasion in 1942 was a possibility. The president did not specify metropolitan France, but the inference was clear. The British were horrified and Roosevelt and his chiefs of staff backed away from what was an incautiously loose bit of talk. They concentrated on *Torch*, the invasion of North West Africa in November which they wished to carry out on their own without any British contribution in the first stages. Churchill meanwhile went to Moscow to tell Stalin that no invasion of Europe was possible in 1942 and to try to persuade him that *Torch* was an equivalent alternative. Churchill left Stalin expecting an invasion of France in 1943 (*Roundup*). Whereas *Sledgehammer* was planned as an act of desperation to be implemented if the Soviet resistance to the German invasion threatened to collapse, *Roundup* was a plan to complement and exploit Soviet success in the east and the consequent denuding by Hitler of his western front. It was regarded with suspicion by cautious service chiefs and although Churchill himself began by believing in it, events – particularly the prolongation of the Tunisian coda to the African campaigns – killed it.

There were two essential preconditions for a cross-Channel invasion in either direction: shipping and command of the air. In 1940 Hitler assembled the shipping but failed in the Battle of Britain to win command of the air and turned away. Besides these two conditions there was the necessary calculation of the likely strength of the defence. In 1942–43 the German army was formidable and planners calculated that in spite of his entanglement in the Soviet Union Hitler might switch 100–200 divisions from east to west: this possibility was not removed until after the battles in the east – in the Ukrainian and White Russian republics – in the summer of 1943. There was – and there has since continued – a brisk debate over the availability of landing craft and other marine transport for *Roundup* or *Overlord*, but more important than the craft were what was to be in them. The one indispensable element was American troops, but in 1942–43 these were neither numerous nor adequately trained (as the North West African venture demonstrated), and there were well-founded worries about transporting these troops not across the Channel but across the Atlantic. The U-boats in the Atlantic were at their most destructive in 1942 and into the next year. The principal weapon against them was the breaking of their Enigma ciphers and from February 1942 the Atlantic U-boats were given a new cipher which Bletchley Park was unable to read until December. In these months sinkings increased alarmingly to a rate of nearly 8 million tons a year, Admiral Doenitz doubled his U-boat fleet and came within sight of his target of 800,000 tons sunk per month, the peak of the U-boats' successes was not reached until the following spring, and 1943 was well advanced before the allies could feel satisfied that the Atlantic was safe enough for the passage of great numbers of men and women and huge quantities of arms and equipment; and the allies had always to reckon with the possibility of French armed resistance to an allied landing – a real possibility so long as Laval had Pétain's ear at Vichy. From the collapse of France in 1940 Churchill had known that victory was not to be achieved without getting the Americans into the war, but that was not all: they had to be got to Europe too and until mid-1943 that problem was unsolved.

Finally, *Overlord* was an extremely hazardous venture. It challenged an enemy greatly superior in numbers; it depended crucially on bizarre untried inventions, on a deception plan which was inherently precarious (although in the event brilliantly successful) and on the weather. It was a leap into the unknown whose failure would have been calamitous for all the allies except possibly Stalin. In Germany, where civilian and military morale were still good and essential parts of war production still rising, Hitler stood to win not only his biggest victory for years but also time for the final development of his V weapons and new submarines of revolutionary design. The mistiming of *Overlord* would have lost the war for its initiators.

The repeated postponements of the Second Front had a source and justification beyond strategic disputes, material strategies and mere confusion. It has frequently been said that war was modernised by the industrial revolution but while this is true of military weapons and doctrines it is less true of the spirit of war. The German Blitzkrieg was acclaimed as the last thing in modern war – the Stuka dive-bomber was its main image – but the spirit of the Blitzkrieg was not so far removed from the spirit of the Light Brigade at Balaclava or the cult of prowess which dominated the warfare of medieval knights and much of the modern officer class. The German military machine annexed technology to bravery and brawn, to numbers and mettle, and proved in 1940 how much better it had done so than the French; and at that stage it needed to do no more. But in Britain and the United States war was being turned into a brainy business. The new science of operations analysis; the invention and testing of bizarre new methods of getting bodies of men from one place to another alive; the acclimatisation of these activities in suspiciously sceptical war offices and fighting units; the harnessing of industrial production and labour to war's needs (badly botched in World War I) – such innovations required a cultural metamorphosis and, by their complexity as well as their novelty, slowed things down. They predisposed leaders not to set operations in motion until they were sure that all was in order and in place. The mood was to get things right first time and then have a go. It was the reverse of having a go and then, if things went wrong, having another go.

World War II may be divided into three (overlapping) phases: the crisis of survival; the fashioning of victory; the contemplation of the future. The first phase passed for Britain with the Battle of Britain, for the Soviet Union with the Battle for Stalingrad. In that phase desperate action might have been justified, but the psychology of survival differs from the psychology of winning, and desperate action has no legitimate place in the latter. *Sledgehammer* marked the transition between these two phases and its successors – *Roundup* and *Overlord* – were planned on the assumption that there was no need to have recourse to desperate remedies. Phase Two was therefore prolonged and Phase Three both delayed and transformed.

Apart from the Soviet Union no continental European state had a leading voice in the postwar settlement of Europe. This was the second dominating factor in the initial reorientation of Europe after World War II and it was a unique occurrence in Europe's history. It was almost as though Europe was being disposed of as Africa had been disposed of at the Congress of Berlin in 1885. Germany having surrendered, the Anglo-Americans on the one hand and the Soviet Union on the other installed pre-arranged joint control by themselves (plus France which was treated as a poor relation but not poor enough to be excluded) but the arrangement did not stick. Joint control was supposed to be a transitional mechanism leading to a more permanent settlement, but the principal victors could not agree on the nature of that settlement and the attempt to do so was abandoned in the winter of 1947–48. The Russians wanted to neuter Germany and to take for themselves what they could in reparations – promises of cash and speedy removal of plants, equipment and other material valuables – but the Americans, having flirted with a similar policy, perceived that if they impoverished Germany they would then have to succour it and on this fundamental disagreement over the central issue of the German economy joint control was laid aside and Germany fell into two sections which graduated to separate states. Stalin accepted this division partly because he had little choice and partly because he preferred total control over part of Germany to shared control in the whole of it. This was the first open and outward sign of the Cold War. It demonstrated that the Soviet armies, although victorious over the German armies, were no match for the American military machine backed by the stupendous and undamaged American arsenal and economy. Stalin limited his ambitions. He established control over what became satellite Europe – in effect a new territorial empire secured and thenceforward guaranteed by Soviet military power but exercised through obedient communist parties. This empire made a brave show on the map and helped to create the myth of two Superpowers, states of a new kind and roughly equal the one with the other. The myth was reinforced when the Soviet Union proved capable of producing nuclear weapons only a few years behind the United States. But maps are not by themselves trustworthy representations of the balance of power.

The partition of Europe extinguished for the duration of the Cold War the concept of Europe as a distinct and autonomous political conglomerate and, since the German Question was how to fit Germany into a European states system, put that question into limbo. But it also accentuated the question by fostering the resurrection of German power with an astonishing and, to many Europeans, disconcerting rapidity. For some of them the most promising answer to the question was to replace the old states system which Germany was bound to dominate by a union in which the rougher edges of domination would be honed by the benefits of entrenched cooperation. Fifty years after the German surrender in 1945 the rouble was worthless and the dollar less sought after than the mark, and the European states system was being replaced by a new political and economic order undreamt of by politicians or economists in 1939. Those who disliked the new order even more than they feared the old system treated it as still a dream; those who welcomed it treated it as more of a reality than it yet was.

. . .

III

Unconditional surrender – and the ensuing Nuremberg trials for which unconditional surrender was a prerequisite – forced Germany, the once and future dominant European Power, to confront its past, re-think the way to satisfy its powers and tailor its ambitions, and espouse radical ideas for Europe's future.

Chapter 2

HESS, UNHESS AND THE PRICE OF PEACE

. . .

I

Rudolf Hess became famous against the grain. He lived most of his adult life in elevated subordination, the subordination being more noticeable than the elevation. He was deputy leader of the Nazi Party and seemed moreover to be one of nature's deputies. But on two occasions, or perhaps one, he stepped into a bigger part – in 1941 and 1987. According to one reading of his life's story he was murdered on both occasions.

In May 1941 he flew from Augsburg in southern Germany to Scotland in an attempt to make peace between Germany and Britain on the eve of the German attack on the Soviet Union. But it has been argued that he never got to Scotland.

In 1946 Rudolf Hess was arraigned before the International Military Tribunal at Nuremberg, convicted and – uniquely – sentenced to be imprisoned for life. This man remained in Spandau prison in Berlin where in 1987 he was found to have committed suicide at the age of ninety-three. But it has been argued that he did not commit suicide but was murdered. In Germany a police investigation opened after his death remains still officially open.

Rudolf Hess was born in Alexandria in 1894. His father had inherited from his father a prosperous merchant business in a prosperous cosmopolitan city. He owned a house on Egypt's Mediterranean coast and another property in the countryside near Munich where the family – father, mother and three children – spent summer holidays. Rudolf went to school in Alexandria and later in Bavaria. He did well. He was an intelligent boy, serious, a touch puritanical. Instead of going from school to university, he took what was probably intended as a loop-line through a course of business studies in Switzerland. Then came World War I.

He fought in France and Romania and was wounded at least three times: first fairly seriously in 1916 in France where he spent a month in hospital and then twice in the next year in Romania. His third wound was severe and landed him in hospital for four months. He did not return to the front. Adrift after the war and disoriented by Germany's defeat, he was deflected from a business or academic career into right-wing politics in which he showed a quiet, unflamboyant but determined and strongly anti-communist commitment. He was for a brief period in one of the Free Corps of demobilised and unemployed officers and men which banded together looking for sustenance or trouble or revenge in postwar Germany and was involved in some haphazard fighting in which he got another slight wound. He went to Munich university, joined the party which was to become the NSDAP (the Nazi Party), met a likeminded girl, Ilse Prohl, whom he subsequently married, but not until 1927 and then, it was said, not without some prompting by Hitler. The only child of the marriage, a son Wolf, was born ten years later. Hitler was a godfather.

Soon after World War I he met the two men who most influenced his life: Adolf Hitler and Professor (previously General) Karl Haushofer, the famous geopolitician from whom he picked up the enthrallingly simple idea that the world would be the better for being divided between Germans and British and run by them in amicable but distant partnership. Haushofer's son Albert became one of Hess's closest friends, but was progressively ambivalent about the Nazis: he was executed by them towards the end of World War II.

To Hitler Hess became fixedly and famously loyal, so much so that Hitler trusted him as he trusted few, if any, people in his motley entourage. Hess was involved in the Hitler–Ludendorf *putsch* of 1923. He escaped arrest when it failed but turned himself in when he learned that Hitler had been arrested and sent to prison. He shared Hitler's imprisonment at Landsberg, near Munich, and there began the close cooperation with the Führer which lasted nearly twenty years. In Landsberg Hitler busied himself writing *Mein Kampf* and Hess helped him.

When Hitler became chancellor of Germany in 1933 he made Hess deputy leader of the Nazi Party, a Reichsminister without Portfolio and third, after Goering, in the government hierarchy. Hess's position was eminent but vague. He was close to Hitler; he was given authority of a kind in both domestic and foreign affairs, particularly in relation to Germans in other countries – the *Volksdeutsche*. He was the least pushy of Hitler's leading barons and he was unlike them too in being a hard-worker and clean-liver. He was also disliked and a little feared: disliked because he was somehow superior in manner, feared because of his inside track to the Führer. His position was coveted by jealous rivals, particularly his own deputy Martin Bormann. He had a weakness for astrologers, but was regarded as otherwise entirely sane and comparatively decent. To the outside world he appeared to have all the qualities required of a number two and none for a number one.

The outbreak of war in 1939 somewhat diminished Hess by contrast with Goering as chief of the Luftwaffe, Goebbels as chief of propaganda and public morale, Germany's leading land and air generals and admirals, and sundry Gauleiters and other party chiefs converted into proconsuls in conquered lands. But for two years Hess remained at the centre of things, working away at whatever Hitler wanted him to do, yet with less to do and more time to brood. He became more and more disturbed and unsettled. He feared a war on two fronts which Germany would lose and the consequent victory of communism which he obsessively detested.[1] He

1. When Hitler made his famous pact with Stalin in August 1939 both men must have had in mind the possibility of a war on two fronts – but a war on two fronts with the Soviet Union as victim, attacked by Germany from the one side and Japan from the other. This did not happen. Hitler, not Stalin, got pincered. Japan, although it joined the Axis in 1940, also concluded in 1941 a non-aggression treaty with the Soviet Union and made war on the United States rather than the Soviet Union. Stalin learned of this choice from the Red Army's spy in Tokyo, Richard Sorge, and so was able to switch forces from his eastern front to the defence of Moscow. The consequences were of the utmost importance, for if Japan had not attacked the United States Hitler would not have declared war on it and the United States would probably not have declared war on Germany. Never had an Asian Power made a greater mark on European history since the Arabs conquered Spain, invaded France and besieged Constantinople.

was convinced that the British must feel the same way about communism but were under the thumb of a Churchillian clique which for some mysterious reason hated Hitler more than communism: in *Mein Kampf* Britain is treated as a natural ally of Germany against the Soviet Union. He must have known that in 1940 some influential British politicians had wanted at least to canvass the possibility of a negotiated peace with Germany and he certainly knew of a number of groups in Germany, some of them anti-Nazi but others within the Nazi Party, who by 1941 were anxious for peace in the west. His close friend Albert Haushofer had contacts with one or more of these groups and dabbled in schemes for secret meetings with British agents in neutral cities – Madrid, Geneva. Some of these schemes entailed getting rid of Hitler and replacing him with another Nazi, the most obvious candidates being Goering and Hess himself. It is a fair conjecture that as the date for the invasion of the Soviet Union approached and the peace-plotters ran into one brick wall after another, Hess became desperate and decided to cast himself as a heroic saviour by going, not to Madrid or Geneva, but to Britain. He would fly to Scotland; land as near as possible to the estate of the Duke of Hamilton, a friend of Haushofer who had been corresponding with him in oblique terms about a peace meeting; and ask to be taken to see King George VI. He wrote explanatory letters to his Führer and his wife to be delivered after his departure. He never saw the Führer again nor his wife for twenty-nine years. He never met the king whom, it seems safe to say, he would have lectured with becoming politeness but in complete ignorance of the monarch's slim influence in British politics.

Hess left Augsburg at 17.45 hours on 10 May 1941 in an Me.110 twin-engined fighter aircraft. A similar aircraft was spotted off the coast of Northumberland at about 22.00 hours. It was a quiet evening both weatherwise and in terms of enemy activity. At first this aircraft was taken to be a Do.215 bomber, an *a priori* judgement based mainly on the assumption that no Me.110 could be in the vicinity since, even if it could reach England, it could not get back to Germany. But more than one member of the vigilant Observer Corps, relying on their own eyes, insisted that it was an Me.110 and an officer of the Corps, dashing to the spot where it crashed, quickly confirmed this identification and noted too that it was brand new and unarmed. For the aircraft, after being plotted across northern England and south-west Scotland as far as the west coast, had turned back and crashed in open country not far from the Duke of Hamilton's seat at Dungavel in Lanarkshire, south of Glasgow. Its remains were scattered over one and a half acres, starting a small fire. The pilot, first reported to have bailed out, failed to jump clear, hurt his ankle on landing, was surrounded by a small posse of the Home Guard and police, declared himself to be Captain Horn and asked to be taken to the duke. He was not amused when his captors laughed, but the Observer Corps officer recognised him as Hess and said so: more laughter.

The news of Hess's departure and arrival caused consternation in Germany and confusion in Britain. The explanations on both sides had one thing in common: Hess was not to be taken seriously. These explanations were designed for immediate propaganda and had nothing to do with the truth of the matter, whatever that might be. Hitler, apparently appalled and furious and fearful of the propagandist opportunities presented to the British by the flight of so eminent a Nazi, summoned a large gathering of Nazi chiefs and Gauleiters to which he read the letter which Hess had caused to be delivered to him and announced that Hess had gone mad. He instructed a reluctant Goebbels to plug this line notwithstanding the damaging questions it must raise about why Hitler had so long employed a madman as his deputy. It was the best he could do by way of damage limitation and he scored by getting his explanation to the world before the British could make up their minds what to say. On the morning of the 13th the BBC was authorised to announce that the deputy Führer had arrived in Britain, piloting his own aircraft and as a solitary refugee from the Gestapo. The British government's view, expounded by Churchill to the House of Commons, was that Hess was perfectly sane but of small consequence. He was to be treated as a prisoner of war captured in uniform, who was also probably a war criminal.

There was at this point no mystery about the prisoner's identity. He was taken to Dungavel where he told the duke he was Hess and emissaries from London had no doubt that he was. Never during his captivity in England nor at Nuremberg at the war's end were any doubts expressed, although, if a later witness is to be believed, Hess was all this time dead. Nor was there any mystery about the prisoner's mission. He had come to see the duke and, through his good offices, the king as an emissary seeking peace between Germany and Britain. This was a story at once simple and plausible and it suffices to explain the suspicions emanating from Moscow where Stalin feared a separate peace in the west to coincide with the opening of a new war in the east. (Stalin urged that Hess be tried at once as a war criminal and the British government prepared a detailed memorandum, to be presented to Stalin by the British ambassador Stafford Cripps, in an attempt to allay Russian suspicions and exculpate itself of complicity in a supposed plan to make peace – which incidentally Britain was at that time fully entitled to do.)

Hess told the Duke of Hamilton that his successful flight had been preceded by three abortive attempts. His accounts of his mission remained thereafter consistent. Hitler, he said, was confident of winning the war, but anxious to stop the slaughter. Hess claimed to know Hitler's mind. He had come to Britain without Hitler's foreknowledge, but with terms for peace which he knew Hitler approved and which he later re-phrased for his interview with the lord chancellor, Lord Simon. After a couple of days in Scotland he was taken under guard to the Tower of London and shortly afterwards to a specially guarded house near Aldershot in the custody of the War Office. This was where it began to be said that he was not quite right in the head and Churchill changed his mind about his sanity and wrote that he should be treated as a medical case. He was for a time deprived of newspapers and radio. He gradually realised that his mission was futile and became depressed to the edge of paranoia. He tried to kill himself. Much of the time he appeared well-informed and alert, but he also exhibited signs, genuine or contrived, of amnesia and had bouts of ill-health. He was visited by the lord chancellor, by Lord Beaverbrook and more than once by the Swiss minister in London. The British ministers tried to get information out of him about Hitler's plans and resources, while he was trying to use them to secure his release from confinement and access to the king. In June 1942 he was moved to another place of confinement in Wales where his general health improved, but his forgetfulness seemed to take greater hold and he made a second attempt at suicide, real or faked. He wrote a great deal – letters and memoranda which, although repetitive, were lucid. There was now serious confusion about his mental condition.

When I was at the Nuremberg trials in 1945–46 there was a lot of puzzled talk about Hess, but nobody ever suggested that the man whom we looked at day after day sitting in the dock between Goering and Ribbentrop was not Hess. Like nearly everybody in the court room I had never seen Hess in the flesh, but I had seen newspaper photographs of him before the war and this man looked like Hess. There was no more reason to suppose him to be an impostor than to query the identity of any of the other men in the dock. That question did not then arise, but another did, a medico-legal one: should this man be standing trial? Was he insane or, even if not insane, of such impaired memory as to be incapable of attending to the proceedings or giving testimony? On that issue there was enough unease to put him into a special category and earn him a unique sentence. When at the end of the trial the judges met to determine their verdicts and sentences, the Russian judges strongly urged that Hess be sentenced to death, but his colleagues dissented and as a compromise Hess was committed to prison for life. Had the Russian view prevailed no question about the prisoner's identity would ever have arisen, but many years later one man came firmly to the conclusion that the man whom we knew at Nuremberg as Hess was not Hess. Let us call him Unhess.

This startling view rests on a single piece of evidence, striking in itself but supported by little else. It is the view of Hugh Thomas, a British army surgeon who happened to be posted to Berlin in 1972 to look after British servicemen. To his surprise he found that his practice included the sole survivor of the war criminals in the city's Spandau prison, and being the sort of man he was he decided to read whatever he could find about this unusual patient with special attention to his medical history. A year or so later he had occasion to examine the prisoner and was transfixed with astonishment: the prisoner could not be Hess. He wrote a book which was published in 1979 and re-published in a revised edition in 1988 as *Hess: A Tale of Two Murders*. Thomas does not write like a man obsessed with a cranky idea, but like one amazed by the evidence of his own eyes. For Thomas, besides reading about Hess's wounds in World War I, had gone to the trouble of getting copies of the contemporary medical records in the German army's archives which showed that Hess's chest and back must bear serious and permanent scars (Mrs Hess later confirmed that this was so). But the prisoner bore no such wounds. When at a later examination Thomas taxed the prisoner with this conundrum he gave signs of extreme distress, even losing control of his bodily functions. Thomas then knew for sure that Rudolf Hess had never reached Scotland.

To say that Thomas was intrigued by his discovery is to put it mildly. Since Hess's departure from Augsburg was incontrovertible – there was even a photograph of it – some very odd questions arose. By his medical observations Thomas had converted a tale of one man into a tale of two, and as he pursued the mystery he came upon bits and pieces which strengthened his view of the case – or at least did not upset it. His investigations need to be read in his own book but, briefly, the most telling items were two: that the aircraft which left Augsburg and the one which landed in Scotland had different markings (i.e. numbers) and that Unhess, although carefully kitted out to resemble Hess, carried none of the documents which Hess could be expected, even obliged, to have about him. Thomas also asked why Unhess, if he were indeed Hess, should have refused to see Mrs Hess until 1969, twenty-eight years after the flight from Augsburg and twenty-three after his arrival in Spandau.

So what happened to Hess and who was Unhess? What was going on if, as the mystery suggested, Hess had been bumped off and Unhess had been sent to Scotland to pursue Hess's mission with Hess out of the way? And why did Unhess preserve his fictional identity for forty-six years even though it landed him in the trial of the century, nearly got him executed and consigned him to prison in Berlin for forty years? For the historian there are not merely two men – Hess and Unhess – but two irreconcilable stories. One of them is simple and consonant with everything we know except that one piece of medical evidence on a body which does not fit it. The other story is fantastic but not easily to be brushed aside. The first story, generally accepted until 1979 and until that date the only one, has Hess setting off for Britain on a mission which has some bizarre aspects but is not inherently implausible, a mission which led to nothing much and was receding into the footnotes of history. There is nothing to tax credulity in this story. Hess could well have done what it requires him to do and he did not need to be mad to do it. The second story is not only more complex but disconcertingly non-existent. The solid ground for it is the denigration of the first story by the revelation of the unscarred body of the prisoner in Spandau whose name, if it was not Rudolf Hess, is unknown and his mission a mere conjecture. This story hangs on a single, albeit not slender, thread and it entails that most suspect of all foundations – conspiracy theory, the last resort of the baffled researcher. There is, however, a little more to it, a twist in its tail, to which we shall come after following Hess from Wales to Nuremberg.

Rudolf Hess was arraigned in 1946 before the International Military Tribunal for the Trial of Major War Criminals. As one-time deputy leader of the Nazi Party he was an almost automatic choice on all counts of the indictment. He was placed in the dock next to Goering, the leading figure among the accused, but before he got there the Tribunal had had to consider his mental state. Hitler had stigmatised him as crazy and so had the British in whose custody he had been for the past five years. Writing a few years after the trial, Churchill maintained that by his flight he had atoned for his crimes (not a strong argument) and was a medical, not a criminal, case. The question for the Tribunal was whether he was mentally fit to stand trial. If he was in legal terms insane, or if he suffered from severe loss of memory, he should not properly be put on trial. The Tribunal appointed a commission of doctors who produced a puzzling and unsatisfactory report, the upshot of which was that he was not unfit to be tried. The Tribunal therefore decided that he should be tried. (The Russians were particularly determined to see him in the dock and saw no very great step between trying him and hanging him.) The prisoner's contribution to this matter was unhelpful. He announced that the amnesia which he had been manifesting during his time in Wales had been tactical and that his only trouble was in concentrating, not in understanding. He said that he had succeeded in deceiving his own counsel (whom he dismissed) and wished to conduct his defence in person. Nervous officers of the court talked him out of this alarming prospect and he accepted a second defence lawyer – who did not make a very good job of an admittedly taxing defence. Hess declared at the outset and again at the last stage of the trial that he accepted responsibility for his actions up to 1941 and his signature on various state documents which were being put in evidence by the prosecution against him: most of them concerned the planning of aggressive wars against Czechoslovakia, Poland, Norway, Holland, Belgium and France.

During much of his trial Hess evinced indifference. He left his headphones off and read what appeared to be novels of no exacting literary or intellectual content. A number of observers commented on this strange behaviour by a man who was after all on trial for his life and must have had at least an inkling that this was so. But did that make him mad? Watching him over the months of the trial I could not come to so clear cut a conclusion. I felt that he was neither mad nor entirely sane, a case which defies standard categories. If he was a maniac he was not the only maniac in the dock. What made him different was his bearing: he was composed, unresponsive, apparently unwilling to treat the proceedings as though they mattered. This was not irrational if, as I thought possible, Hess had come to the conclusion that his fate was decided. He had failed to get a hearing in England and had no hope of faring better in an international criminal court. He might as well give up, pay minimal attention to what was going on amid pointlessly prolonged lawyers' chatter, and present a front of polite disdain. Telford Taylor, the American deputy chief of counsel whose book *The Anatomy of the Nuremberg Trials* (New York, 1992) is the outstanding record of the trials and their antecedents, records a telling incident. Taylor, half listening to a speech by one of his colleagues, noticed that the speaker made a slip in referring to the relative positions of Goering and Hess in the Reich hierarchy. He quickly looked towards the dock and noted not only that Goering was gesticulating indignantly against the error, but that Hess too had heard it and was looking at Goering with a mischievous grin: for the American lawyer had put Hess a notch above Goering instead of the other way round. So for part of the time at least Hess was more acute than he gave himself out to be. But he was odd and I gradually came to the conclusion that his oddness was not mere play-acting. It was consistent over the best part of a year. He did not go into the witness box – he was dissuaded by his counsel from doing so – and observers did not have the opportunity of judging him under the peculiar stresses of examination and cross-examination, but he was allowed at the end of the proceedings to make a final speech. It was an embarrassing affair, a rambling and sometimes incoherent survey of the German predicament from the Treaty of Versailles onwards which the presiding judge, Lord Justice Lawrence, tolerated for some time even when Goering tried to make Hess sit down. Finally Lawrence ordered him to conclude which, in a startling change of style, he did with a clear and dignified statement of his pride in what he had done for Germany and his faith in Hitler. After that performance no sane person could have judged him totally sane. Taylor's final verdict is that he should not have been put on trial nor put in prison for the rest of his life and that would be my verdict too.

The Tribunal's judgment makes embarrassing reading at this point. It ruled that Hess's behaviour was abnormal but no worse. It found him guilty on the charges against peace, but not guilty of war crimes or crimes against humainty and, in what was in effect a compromise between the Russians and the rest of the bench, imposed its unique sentence of life imprisonment. He was despatched to Spandau, a nineteenth-century gaol in the British sector of Berlin which had once housed 600 inmates but was refurbished to take seven. These were, besides Hess: von Neurath, Raeder, Doenitz, Funk, Schirach, Speer. All but Hess were released during the 1950s and 1960s, leaving Hess as the only inmate from 1966 to his death in 1987. In the later years appeals for his release, including appeals from heads of state in the United States, Britain and France, failed to move the Russians and he was never released. He attempted suicide in 1977. Ten years on the world learned that at the age of ninety-three Hess was at last dead and by his own hand by hanging.

Enter once more Hugh Thomas. According to Thomas the prisoner of Spandau was by the 1980s incapable of hanging himself because enfeebled and deformed. Thomas produced evidence to show that he was murdered by a blow to the back of the head and by strangulation. There were two *post mortems*, one conducted by the four-Power authority in Berlin and the second on behalf of the family when the body was delivered to them for burial. Their findings are incompatible with one another and with the official announcement of death by hanging. In Britain questions in parliament received from ministers in the Thatcher government replies which were evasive and looked untrue. Devotees of conspiracy theory concluded that there was still something to hide. There was also a new mystery. Why after all these years and on the verge of death had Unhess too been bumped off?

.   .   .

II

When Hess set out for Britain in May 1941 Germany was within weeks of making war on the Soviet Union. Hess's escapade has always been regarded as an attempt to bring the war between Germany and Britain to a negotiated end and there is no reason to dispute this view. Not only is Hess known to have been dabbling in schemes with this object, but at Nuremberg his counsel produced the outline of a plan which Hess addressed to the English lord chancellor, Lord Simon. In this plan Hess proposed a four-point basis for peace: first, that the world be divided into two spheres of interest, Europe as the domain of the Axis allies and the British empire as the domain of Great Britain; second (and nevertheless), that Britain return Germany's former colonies; third, that German and British citizens damaged during or before the war be indemnified; and fourth, that Italy be simultaneously included in an armistice and peace between Germany and Britain. That, apparently, was the way Hess was thinking. As a way of detaching Britain from the war the plan had scant prospect of success, but presumably Hess believed otherwise. From the British point of view it left Germany in control of all of continental Europe, a situation which more than any other had induced Britain to contemplate and then embark on war. Secondly, the British imperial sphere would be severely constrained if French as well as British ex-German colonies were to be returned to

Germany and if France, Belgium and other European states in the German sphere of interest were to forfeit to Germany (as European overlord) some degree of control over their non-German colonies: in sum, a considerable diminution of British power beyond as well as within continental Europe. But this back-of-an-envelope proposal could be regarded as no more than an invitation to discuss, not a very subtle invitation but at least an overture demanding a sequel and behind it lay the larger concept of an Anglo-German con-dominion such as had been around in England as well as Germany before the end of the previous century. There were plenty of people in both countries who had flirted with the notion that the British and Germans together amounted to something like a superior race. Yet on the most favourable view of Anglo-German relations anything like the Hess plan of 1941 was a non-starter. It ignored the fact that quite apart from the enormities of Hitler in recent years Anglo-German relations had reached and passed their best half a century earlier. Britain had come to fear German power as an instru-ment for the subjugation of a continental Europe of which Britain, however eccentrically, was a part. The prime issue in both World Wars was the power of Germany, not the behaviour or ideology of its government. That Hess and perhaps Hitler too could think of opening discussions with Britain with proposals which evicted it from continental Europe testifies to their comprehensive incomprehension or, in the case of Hitler, relative indifference to the British response. Yet there were in Britain some who might be dis-posed to listen to more realistic proposals.

They had done so a year earlier, when the British cabinet had discussed making approaches to Mussolini and to Hitler. The object of approaching Mussolini was to discover his price for keeping out of the war (in much the same spirit as his predecessors in World War I had been paid for coming in to it) and this object was especially close to the hearts of the ailing French. Nothing came of this idea. Nor did any-thing come of proposals to put out feelers to Hitler. For the British at this date the war had hardly begun, its initial encounters with Norway, the Low Countries and France were depressing and Hitler was judged (correctly as it turned out) to be keener on rounding off his successes in the west by peace with Britain than on invading it. But Britain could

embark on negotiations only from a position of acknowledged weakness and by renouncing its principal war aims,
and although the cabinet was divided Churchill's staunch
opposition prevailed over the waverers. A year later the situation had changed in some respects but not in a crucial
one. Hitler remained unenthusiastic about war with Britain
(although unafraid of it) and his inclination to tidy up western Europe was fortified by his resolve to invade the Soviet
Union that summer. Britain had won the Battle of Britain
but still had small reason to expect American military participation in the war. Britain might get in 1941 better terms
than it could have expected in 1940, but it had small reason
– and Hess's mission confirmed this calculation – to suppose that Hitler would settle for anything which did not
leave him dominant over continental Europe. Churchill, who
was more firmly in control of the government in 1941 than
in 1940, remained inexorably opposed to negotiation, an
attitude which has generally been ascribed to his character
but was not devoid of more rational calculation.

The essential difference between Churchill and his adversaries on this issue was that he had a simple war aim and only
one. His aim was to win and to do so unequivocally. This
simplistic purpose was one of his strengths. The switch from
Chamberlain to Churchill in 1940 was the installation of a
man with a purpose in place of a man at a loss for a purpose. Because Chamberlain had no definable war aims he
and his like could the more easily give up the war. Chamberlain had devoted himself to preventing the war. Under-
standably and honourably, he flinched from declaring a
war in which, while he himself would be too old to serve at
the front, hundreds of thousands of young people would be
killed. It was a difficult and perhaps impossible endeavour
and he bungled it. He deluded himself too easily and for
too long into believing that he could deserve well of his
country and the world by talking peace with Hitler who was,
however, a man who did not flinch from war and had said
so. Hitler had a single inflexible purpose which was the
territorial aggrandisement of Germany and it was unattain-
able without war. Chamberlain and Hitler were always talking at cross-purposes since for Chamberlain the issue was
peace or war while for Hitler the question was about ways
and means, not purpose. There were, of course, things which

Chamberlain would never concede, but it was not clear what these things were; he did not formulate a policy with markers to delimit the areas of permissible discussion. The man who professes a willingness to talk anywhere at any time is most often a man at sea.

Chamberlain wanted to 'stop' Hitler. His method was to talk Hitler out of seizing other countries' territory and meet Germany's just grievances. But these were not the point. Germany had grievances which derived from the Treaty of Versailles, but Hitler had also ambitions which had nothing to do with Versailles. The grievances had served to help Hitler win power, but redressing them was not Hitler's essential aim. Although in detail and timing Hitler's intentions were vague or at least flexible, his main aim – which again he had set out clearly and publicly in *Mein Kampf* – was concrete: to seize land which would give Germany not only rich resources but dominance over Europe. On this issue Hitler was unbiddable and in that fact lies the condemnation of the policy of appeasement of the 1930s since it involved letting Hitler and Germany have something which in the end the rest of Europe could not afford to let them have. Chamberlain was looking for an acceptable price to pay for preventing war, but there was no such price. Hitler was prepared to take anything which he might be offered – at Munich, for example – and then fight for the rest of what he wanted. Churchill was always distrustful of the game which Chamberlain was playing with Hitler's Germany and he had the advantage of watching it from the outside. When war came and he became prime minister his mind was unbefogged. Hitler and Germany could be stopped only by their defeat.

Chamberlain died at the end of 1940. He was survived by a number of senior politicians who shared his outlook and, like him, held office in Churchill's cabinet. They were alert to the possibilities of peace – but less so to the consequences. In the early summer of 1940, with France about to be overwhelmed and Italy about to extend the war to the Mediterranean, Halifax, Butler and other Conservatives of the older and younger generations asked if it made sense to go on fighting. They wanted to probe the possibilities of a peace which, without too much obloquy and humiliation, would save lives, resources and Britain's imperilled position in Europe and the world. They were also moved by distrust of Churchill personally. For his part Churchill would have none of it. His priorities were different. He judged that the aggrandisement of Germany, postponed in 1914–19, must be scotched, that Hitler must not be allowed to turn continental Europe into a German estate (as Bonaparte had famously added Genoa and Lucca, and much more, to his family estate). He may not have counted the cost or foreseen it, for he was not a counting man. The historical point is that his view prevailed, narrowly in 1940 but virtually effortlessly in 1941. In 1938–40 Hitler had conquered or absorbed eight independent countries and in 1941 he was addressing confidently the ultimate item of invading and destroying the USSR. There is no reason to suppose that Churchill would have opposed appeasement either before or during the war if he had judged that this menacing German programme might thereby have been stopped, but he did not believe that – and surely correctly. He was probably in favour of the destruction of the USSR (had that been on the agenda), but not its destruction by Hitler. Therefore going to war had been right and going on with the war in spite of disasters and the prospect of worse to come was also right.

Churchill's attitude has been represented as the triumph of emotion over reason – a lucky triumph if that is the right way to judge the conflict between the would-be peacemakers and those who were resolved to dig in their heels. But to dramatise this conflict as one between reason and unreason is superficial and wrong. Halifax, Butler and their like were reasoning on grounds narrowed by hopelessness. They were short on vision. To include vision in calculations is dangerous, but sometimes appropriate and the crises of 1940 and 1941 were occasions when it was not only appropriate in retrospect but justified. There was, however, one chink in this broader calculation. Suppose that Hitler could be got rid of. Was that a possibility and what difference would it make? There are short answers to these questions: the possibility was remote and the difference would be slight. Attempts were made over the next few years to kill Hitler but none succeeded – he killed himself. More to the point was the answer to the second question. Making peace in 1941, on Hess's terms or anything like them, entailed substituting one Nazi leader for another. It did not entail changing

German policy, least of all the impending invasion of Russia, and it would do little or nothing to curb Germany's power or ambitions in Europe: the Hess plan did not even pretend to do so, for it was a plan to entrench Germany's dominance of the continent with British consent and to banish British power to beyond the seas. Therefore Hess and whoever may have been behind him were in 1941, like the British peace-makers in 1940, on a hiding to nothing. In neither case was there a response from the other side, or not more than the feeblest tinkle. To the Peace Question the answer was No.

The questions which remain are intriguing but subordinate. Did anybody in Britain have an inkling about Hess's escapade? The Secret Service? Chamberlainites? Churchill himself? Hess, or Unhess, was quickly tucked away in one safe house or another, but that is not very surprising.

If Hess was not Hess, what happened to Hess? The ingenious Thomas suggests, not entirely without evidence, that he was shot down with malice aforethought over the North Sea on that May evening in 1941 on Goering's orders. Hess was not a man for whom many tears need be shed, but if he did reach Scotland and eventually Nuremberg, then he was harshly treated at Nuremberg and for longer thereafter than conscience can comfortably accept.

And who was Unhess? He has no name, which is one of the oddest parts of his story. In stories of this kind there are usually too many candidates, not too few. Thomas surmises that he was a double of Hess picked up and used by Goering or Himmler as part of a conspiracy to get rid of Hess and Hitler. Unhess made a reasonably good impersonator with occasional lapses. He seems, for example, to have stopped being a vegetarian, to have had poorer table manners than Hess and to have known strangely little about Hess's favourite game of tennis. But perhaps, being or becoming Hess, he had forgotten these things. The most bizarre questions about Unhess are why he should keep silent about his identity after the war and why he should have been murdered. If, as Thomas proposes, he was blackmailed by Himmler, he would have played his allotted role until 1945 but why after Himmler's death and the total collapse of the SS and the entire Nazi state? For his supposed murder Thomas's guess is that in old age his wits deserted him, he began to ramble

41

and had to be silenced. But by whom? The finger points at the Russians or the British, unconvincingly.[2]

The Russians were particularly vengeful about Hess. They insisted on his being put on trial at Nuremberg and pressed for him to be condemned to death. They hated or feared him. The simplest explanation is that they associated him with attempts to end the war in the west and leave the Soviet Union to face Hitler's armies on its own. This reasoning assigns to Britain's continuing belligerence a greater consequence for the Soviet Union than Russians habitually admitted. Stalin was perenially suspicious of plans for a separate peace in the west and he had most cause for alarm as the inescapability of *Barbarossa* and his incapacity to meet it dawned upon him, but whether he had any concrete knowledge of concrete plots we do not know. He is unlikely to have drawn distinctions between Churchill and the Chamberlainites since Churchill was more renowned than any Chamberlainite for hostility to the Bolshevik Revolution. That the British were embarrassed and confused by the sudden arrival of Hess in Scotland is in retrospect fairly clear, and not particularly sinister. It was precisely the sort of incident which has people running round in circles but such behaviour is not enough to warrant the assumption that the British had some muddy tracks to cover. Of such a line of argument William of Ockham would not have approved: *entia non sunt multiplicanda praeter necessitatem* (propositions should not be unnecessarily multiplied or, more simply, do not complicate an argument in order to get the answer you want).

I do not know for certain when or where Rudolf Hess died and I do not know whether there was an Unhess or not. I would like to know the answers to these questions because they are intriguing. But I am content not to know because their historical importance is slight.

Contrariwise, however, the question whether Britain and Germany could and should have made peace in 1941 is a question of the very greatest significance. Had they done so millions of lives would have been saved. There would have been no Holocaust and no state of Israel. The probable

2. Hugh Thomas later wrote another book which challenged the accepted view on the deaths of Hitler and Eva Braun, *Doppelgangers: The Truth about the Bodies in the Berlin Bunker* (London, 1995).

– but not certain – downfall of the Soviet Union with the extinction of the Gulag would have saved more lives and misery. Britain would have survived the war stronger and wealthier than it did in 1945 and the United States would not have come into the war in Europe. On the other hand the Nazi regime in Germany or something very like it would have survived and flourished and so, for a time at least, would have fascism in Italy. France must have complied, to some extent willingly, with these vicious forms of right-wing politicians on the continent. Even for Britain, the superficially obvious beneficiary of an early peace, the balance is not easily weighed. Britain would have found it relatively easy and undoubtedly enticing to try to maintain in the world an imperial stance which was already slipping. A peace in 1941 – again assuming the defeat of the Soviet Union by Germany fighting on one front only – would be a victory for Hitler and for his conception of Europe as a continent with a single overlord, Germany. From this Europe, economically menacing and ideologically repulsive, Britain would have been isolated. For good or ill, there would have been few Americans around apart from corporation executives doing deals with German industrial giants or shaping a super-military-industrial complex: Wall Street without Gettysburg.

The war which might just possibly have been ended in 1941 was a European war and if it had ended then Europe would have become what Hess and Hitler wanted it to be – a place unfit for others to live in. It is hard for a survivor to say that all those others who did not survive had to die. But so it was in 1941. Wars are not entered upon lightly. You go to war with a purpose and given the nature of war that purpose must be seriously pondered, calculated and maintained. And it should be abandoned or compromised voluntarily only if you come to the conclusion that you have gravely overestimated its importance or gravely underestimated the cost of achieving it.

. . .

III

Rudolf Hess personified the policy, by no means confined to Germans, of striking a deal between democratic and fascist states in order to confront and possibly fight the Soviet

Union which, besides being feared for its great size and unassessable power, was the fount and patron of European communism in the twentieth century. There had been a moment when fascism and communism, represented by Hitler and Stalin, seemed intent on striking a different deal but Hitler never meant it. (Nor did he mean to create the Soviet-American alliance which undid him.) The war against Germany was not chosen by the democracies in preference to a war against the Soviet Union. It was provoked by Hitler and the democracies did their best to avoid it. From the democratic point of view there was no moral preference between Hitler and Stalin, but in practice and as things turned out war against Germany came first and once embarked on that war it made no sense to stop it halfway through in order to embark on another – with the Nazis but without the United States. Hard on the conclusion of the World War, war on the Soviet Union followed in the peculiar mode called the Cold War which lasted much longer but killed fewer people and left Germany – a democratic Germany – the most powerful state in Europe once more.

Chapter 3

DRESDEN: WAR, LAW AND MORALITY

. . .

I

On 13–14 January 1945 the city of Dresden was attacked and extensively destroyed by RAF Bomber Command and the US Eighth Air Force. The main night attack by Bomber Command came in two distinct operations comprising 800 sorties and elaborately supported by the most sophisticated technical equipment, widespread diversionary attacks and deception. The British attacks were followed by an American daylight raid. The combined operations lasted fourteen hours, from 22.15 hours to nearly midday on the following day. No German fighters and little anti-aircraft fire hindered the attackers, only three of which were shot down. The Luftwaffe's day and night fighters had been knocked out of the war in the preceding months and the city's anti-aircraft defences dispersed to other parts of Germany and to the eastern front. The number of the dead was around 35,000 plus an incalculable number incinerated not merely beyond recognition but beyond identification as human beings. It was a highly competent performance and the culmination of one of the war's longest, heaviest and costliest campaigns: almost a war within a war. The aim of this campaign was the capitulation of Germany through the destruction of its cities, its war economy and its morale. The raid on Dresden did not by itself achieve that aim, but a few months later similar raids on two Japanese cities (albeit with bombs of a terrifying novel kind) led to the immediate capitulation of Japan.

The destruction of Dresden was both an item in a campaign and by virtue of its extreme dreadfulness an independent symbolic horror. The death toll, the extent of the damage, the fame and beauty of the city and its defencelessness combined to stir revulsion and outrage and make of this particular incident a focus of the senseless brutality of war, especially air war. It has been excoriated by two groups: those who distinguish the weapons and tactics of mass destruction and demand that they be more clearly outlawed, and those who condemn modern war *in toto* as incompatible with civilisation.

The bombing of Dresden was the logical outcome of a theory which maintained that wars may be won by air power alone. The theory was dear to airmen. The armed services of states have, historically and characteristically, been led by men of professional keenness and competitiveness who – when not employed in overthrowing or bullying civilian governments as they habitually do in many parts of the world – have employed much of their energies in denigrating one another. The emergence of air power in the twentieth century made these conflicts triangular and airmen, as the new boys, had the hardest row to hoe. They became more assertive than army generals and much more assertive than admirals. It is, however, ungracious and superficial to depict them as no more than selfish in-fighters or cowboys in uniforms. Their claims to have overtaken the admirals and generals were not entirely hollow, although frequently pressed with self-serving exaggeration. There was, first, the experience of World War I. The surrender of Germany in 1918 was clearly not brought about by the British navy whose great ships did practically nothing to the German High Seas fleet except confront it (when not missing it) on one day and night in May 1916. The German armies were indeed forced to surrender, but afterwards maintained that they had done so not because they were defeated by opposing armies, but because of the collapse of German civilian morale (which in the next war was made a prime target of air forces). The impact of air power remained ambiguous because it was still embryonic; it was not found wanting because it was only marginally deployed and in the years between the wars it was not unreasonable to argue that future wars could be shortened and won by air attacks on enemy morale and industries: that was one of the definitions of modern war. Instead of confronting one another, armed forces would directly attack the enemy's will to fight and his economic capacity to do so. The motto of the more optimistic airmen was: Leave it to us. To which might be added *sotto voce*: And don't get in the way. They might even in the jargon of a different trade claim to be cost effective and in riposte to moralists they could assert that the air warfare pioneered in World War I was no more horrible or inhumane than trench warfare. The symbols of the horrors of war were the Somme and Passchendaele, not the cavortings of intrepid young men in flying machines. What nobody knew, because it was still the sci-fi of the times, was what air power would do in World War II.

Air Marshal Arthur Harris, who was appointed commander-in-chief of Bomber Command early in 1942, was a stout protagonist of the extreme claims for air power, as his post demanded. So too was his superior Air Chief Marshal Sir Charles Portal, chief of the air staff and one of Harris's predecessors at Bomber Command. (He was its commander-in-chief for six months during 1940.) Winston Churchill was sometimes of their way of thinking, but neither consistently nor wholeheartedly. He would sometimes seize on the idea of strategic bombing, in which he was supported by his trusted scientific adviser Professor Lindemann (later Lord Cherwell), a fervent bombomaniac; but he had more faith than airmen or scientists in the stoutheartedness of the civilian population and saw no reason to suppose that German civilians were less brave or less resolute than British.

Circumstances conspired to incline Churchill to put a large part of his trust in bombing. At Casablanca in January 1943, when he and Roosevelt and their service chiefs met to decide what to do next after the Germans and Italians were cleared out of Africa, he espoused the combined Anglo-American bombing of Germany. A gap was looming between the end of the African campaign and an invasion of northern France. This gap was envisaged as perhaps six or seven months during which the Russians would be fighting for their survival and their allies had to find something useful to do (the gap extended to eighteen months but that was unexpected). There was talk of seizing Sicily or Sardinia or both as staging posts to the Italian mainland, but to the Americans and, above all, to the Russians these adventures would not sufficiently engage Hitler's ground forces or relieve the Russians still fighting desperately on the Volga at Stalingrad. The weapon which lay readily to hand was the heavy bomber. The first American raid into Germany by heavy bombers was made that month.

Bomber Command had started the war with inadequate and ineffective aircraft whose operations were too often suicidal for its crews who failed by miles to hit their targets and failed to return safely to base. But during 1942 the Command was transformed by the advent of the four-engined bomber, new and weightier high explosive bombs and incendiaries, and a new commander-in-chief, and it had begun to impose itself on the fortunes of war by heavy raids on coastal cities (Lübeck, Rostock) and the so-called Thousand Bomber raid on Cologne: the last was a sign of things to come if not an accurate description of what it was. The big claims made for the independent use of air power to win a war looked for the first time plausible. By 1943 the question was not whether to give strategic bombing a main role but how. Bomber Command was, to use an anachronistic colloquialism, on a roll.

There were, however, differences over what to bomb. Harris put his faith in bombing cities – that is to say, people and their houses: it was called, for short, de-housing. He did so not because he was unnaturally keen on killing people or because he thought German morale fragile, but because his forces could not yet destroy smaller targets except at unacceptable cost in lives and machines: the dambuster raid of May 1943 proved the point. The balance of power between the defending night fighters and the night bomber still lay with the former. Although the bombers could get through, they either inflicted too little damage or did not get back. At Casablanca the service and political chiefs produced a directive giving priority to the destruction of oil installations, the aircraft industry and U-boat havens, but Harris ignored it as much as he could (which was most of the time) and continued to demonstrate the effectiveness of air power by bombing German cities. (Although nobody knew it until after the war German industry was not overstretched, so that even if the bombers had been able to hit precise targets there was spare capacity available to fill gaps in production. Speer won fame not by miracles but by skilful use of spare capacity.)

In 1944 Harris did what he was required to do in bombing transport targets and communications in preparation for

Overlord. He complied against the grain. He did not believe that *Overlord* would succeed. He even doubted whether it would get off the ground. In the same months Harris's campaign against cities became spectacular and irreversible with the aid of new techniques such as improved aiming devices and the metal strips called Window which confused radar defences. The sheer volume of the attacks increased their destructiveness by more than the added weight of explosives, for it created the firestorms which incinerated tens of thousands of people who were unable to run away fast enough.[1] In Hamburg at least 40,000 civilians were killed and half the survivors fled the city. Berlin was bombed sixteen times over four months during the winter of 1943–44.

The programme was interrupted by the need for operations in direct support of the landings in Normandy, but it was no more than interrupted and was resumed and extended as city after city hitherto immune came within the range of Bomber Command. Towards the end of 1944 Harris claimed that he had virtually destroyed all but fifteen of Germany's largest cities (100,000 inhabitants or more) and was ready to destroy the rest. Most of these were in Saxony which, as the Russians crossed the Oder instead of taking a winter's rest, was in imminent danger of invasion first by refugees and then by the Red Army. Harris regarded attacks on other targets as distractions. He received in September 1944 a fresh directive which kept oil installations as his Command's first priority, with communications (rail and inland waterways), tank production, ordnance factories, motor transport production and depots next, but he went his own way as far as he could and at the cost of some painful brushes with Portal which the latter refrained from pursuing to the point where Harris could have been forced to resign or be dismissed. A further directive from the chiefs of staff in January 1945 – *Operation Thunderclap* – unleashed Bomber Command over a wide area from Berlin eastward. The Command itself chose its targets night by night.

1. The term 'firestorm' was coined after the raid on Hamburg on 5 June 1943. A firestorm is an intensification of natural processes. Burning buildings create temperatures which suck in hot air which scatters burning fragments which start more fires which raise yet higher temperatures which create currents of storm velocity and temperatures of 800 degrees centigrade.

The Casablanca directive of January 1943 had spoken of the strategic offensive as a combined Anglo-American operation, but there had been little cooperation so far mainly because the Americans persisted with the hazardous strategy of daytime bombing with heavy bombers which relied for their safety on being heavily armoured instead of being escorted by fighters up to and over their targets. They risked fearful casualties in order to achieve precision and until the end of 1943 the equation worked wretchedly against them. While the German night fighters were still holding their own against Bomber Command, the German day fighters were more than holding their own against the US Eighth Air Force. But the balance shifted abruptly when the Americans found a fighter, the Mustang, which could escort the bombers all the way and outmanoeuvre German fighters too. In the first half of 1944 the Germans lost the daytime battle of the air and the Americans began to be able to bomb precise targets at acceptable cost to themselves. After the war General Galland, chief of staff of the Luftwaffe, said that Hitler's gamble in the Ardennes at the end of 1944 finally killed off the Luftwaffe. The way was clear for the kind of cooperation foreshadowed at Casablanca. The logical next step for Bomber Command and the logical next step for the Eighth Air Force came together.

When the commanders of the two forces considered the furtherance of their instructions to reduce the German will to fight they hesitated to include Dresden in their list of prime targets. (Nagasaki too was a dubious choice until the last moment when it was substituted for Kyoto, considered too sacred.) Dresden had been the capital of the electors and kings of Saxony whose rule, which lasted into living memory, ended with the abdication of the last king in 1918. Largely rebuilt in the eighteenth century, it was one of the showpieces of European late Baroque architecture. It had suffered two minor raids, but was substantially undamaged and its citizens were more worried about the flood of refugees from the east and the approach of the fearsomely intemperate Russian soldiery than by any threat of British or American bombardment from the air. Dresden was not an open city in the sense that Rome had been declared an open city but it was industrially insignificant and the railways which ran through it were secondary: in both respects

Dresden was less important than other Saxon cities such as Leipzig or Chemnitz and, in terms of both strategy and law, in a different category from the great industrial cities of the Ruhr. The authorities had not thought it necessary to provide air raid shelters. No sirens sounded.

In his Lees Knowles lectures at Cambridge in 1963[2] Dr Noble Frankland, who knew at first hand what it was like to fly as a navigator in Bomber Command and after the war wrote (with Professor C.K. Webster) the official history of the British bombing offensive against Germany, argued pertinently that each operation has to be judged in its context. In relation to Dresden he cited three special circumstances. The first was the urge to deliver a massive blow against Germany because the drive to victory on the western front had slackened during the winter and because there was an uneasiness about new German weapons which had come, or were coming, into service: the V weapons, jet aircraft, the Schnorkel on U-boats. The second was the need to help the westward march of the Russian armies, and the third was the natural human determination always to go one better than last time – in this case to choose targets at an even greater range than any previously attacked by the Command. I would add a fourth circumstance of which I had personal knowledge at the time: the argument that Dresden was the rail junction through which important German forces were about to pass. Frankland judged in 1963 that even when these circumstances were taken into account the attack on Dresden was questionable. Thirty years later it seems to me unquestionably indefensible.

The V 1 and V 2 came into use in the summer and autumn of 1944. They were alarming weapons but they came too late. The V 1 attack on England lasted only a few months and the V 2 attack against London was mastered by the end of 1944 (it continued for a time against Antwerp). The new U-boats were so severely bombarded in their factories and pens throughout 1944 that none ever fired a torpedo in anger. The allies were reasonably informed about the development and progress of jet aircraft, fighters and bombers, and satisfied that they posed no imminent threat.

---

2. Subsequently published as *The Bombing Offensive against Germany* (London, 1965).

As the western and eastern allies converged on Germany arrangements were made for the former to facilitate the advance of the latter. These arrangements consisted in the reporting of 'battle lines' and requests from the Russian side for ancillary action by British and American forces. I recall no such request in relation to Dresden and have never been able to find any trace of one, nor do I believe that the western commanders ever debated ways of helping the Russians unless first asked specifically to do so. They did not see it as part of their business to intervene unsolicited. I do not believe that there was any thought of the Russians in the minds of the British and Americans when they were planning the Dresden raids.

Frankland's third point is valid. Commanders embarked on a campaign are naturally keen to push it to its practical and tactical limits, but that does not mean that there are no limits of another kind. The western bomber commanders were instructed by their superiors to bombard Germany and in doing so they selected targets and deployed resources as they saw fit. They had choices and in choosing they were under an obligation to consider not only tactical and strategic matters, but also the laws of war. What they chose to do to Dresden was legally – and morally – indefensible. Before examining these matters I shall insert a personal note on the surrounding circumstances as I saw them at the time.

In February 1945 I was the head of a section of Hut 3 at Bletchley Park whose business it was to interpret and disseminate intelligence derived from the interception and decipherment of the Luftwaffe's high grade ciphers – the intelligence called Ultra. In this position I was in regular and frequent touch by telephone, sometimes several times a day, with intelligence officers in the Air Ministry in London and elsewhere and in even closer touch with colleagues handling German army traffic of the same kind – they were in fact just across the corridor in the same Hut. One of our main concerns in early February was the whereabouts and intentions of the Sixth SS Panzer Army commanded by SS General Sepp Dietrich. This Army had been transferred from east to west for Hitler's offensive in the Ardennes in December 1944 and after its rebuff was on its way back to the east. The question was by what route. There were some *a priori* grounds for supposing that it might go via Dresden but no hard evidence that it would. Although Dresden was not a major rail centre it was virtually undamaged and if Sixth SS Panzer could be caught there the station and its surroundings would be not only a legitimate target but also one well worth hitting. Our information at Bletchley Park was that it was not going through Dresden. The day before the proposed raid I got a call from the Air Ministry – from, as it happened, my predecessor in Hut 3 – who wanted to know if I was certain that Sixth SS Panzer was not being routed through Dresden. As he sounded particularly concerned I asked him what was up. He replied that Dresden was to be heavily attacked and the movements of Sixth SS Panzer were the pretext. He said that if I were entirely certain of what I had told him he would get on to the allied air commanders and tell them that these grounds for bombing Dresden were not valid. I reiterated that we now knew what the orders to the Army were but, as usual, could not rule out the possibility, however unlikely, that these orders could be changed or cancelled by telephone or by other means not open to Ultra intelligence. Later he told me that the commander-in-chief of the Eighth Air Force had been willing to call off the raid provided that the commander-in-chief of Bomber Command, with whom he was concerting the operation, would do so too; but at Bomber Command the commander-in-chief had not been available and his deputy had not been willing to cancel the operation in his superior's absence and at such short notice. At this distance in time I doubt whether the movements of Sixth SS Panzer were a principal element in the bombing of Dresden. It would have been convenient if Sixth SS Panzer had been routed through Dresden and it is certain that before and after the raid its movements were talked about in that connection. There was also some uneasiness which was not confined to lily-livered bishops. Churchill expressed it privately a few weeks later.

To the commander-in-chief of Bomber Command arguments of this kind must have seemed tiresomely irrelevant or worse. Harris's first aim was to destroy German cities. His policy was, in his own terms, successful: cities were being destroyed. There were still a number to be destroyed. Harris was sure that he was helping in a big way to win the war and end it sooner rather than later; he was conscious of a need to assert and defend himself against critics who wanted him to use his force in ways which he, its commander, deemed mistaken; and he was a man of stubborn temper, with more resolve than reflectiveness, proud to the point of enjoying defiance. Which of these factors played the greater part in setting the course of events it is pointless to inquire. About the morality of what he did he may have had qualms and posterity will hesitate to judge: moral questions seldom receive precise answers. Law, however, is more precise and the law – to which Harris almost certainly paid scant attention – must condemn his action on this particular occasion.

. . .

II

About the morality of strategic or mass bombing little will be said here. For some moralists all war is immoral and to distinguish between moral and immoral acts of war is to blur the main issue. Others accept war as an inescapable human activity and try to humanise it by proposing rules to govern it. Such rules derive their immediate force from law, but they draw ultimate sanction from moral precept.

It is easy but superficial to assert that morality does not come into public affairs. The truth is more complex. Morality does encroach into public and corporate affairs, but only feebly. All these matters are conducted by human beings and human beings are endowed with a sense of right and wrong. Where this sense comes from is one of those questions which have been debated for centuries without conclusive answer, but the persistence of the debate demonstrates both the validity of the question and the sharpness of the dilemma which it exposes: the conflict between public or corporate duty and personal morality. An individual may be asked to sanction or condone behaviour which in a personal context he would unhesitatingly condemn and refuse. In the fifth century BC the Athenian admiral Themistocles, who had just won the Battle of Salamis which saved Greece from becoming a Persian satrapy, disclosed that he knew how to make Athens permanently supreme among the Greek city states but could not make up his mind whether he should render this supreme service to his city because his plan was as dishonourable as it was certain of success. So, says Plutarch who tells this story in his life of Themistocles, he publicly bared his soul and asked for guidance. He was told to explain his plan privately to the famously good Aristides who vetoed it on moral grounds: it consisted in destroying in harbour all the ships of the allies who had helped the Athenians to sink the Persian fleet at Salamis. Aristides then reported the situation to his fellow citizens who applauded his decision. (They subsequently exiled him for being too good by half.) Two and a half thousand years later, in the 1930s, Henry L. Stimson, US secretary of state, discovered that his office was successfully deciphering the codes used by friendly countries. He ordered that the practice be stopped on the grounds that gentlemen do not read one another's correspondence. Whether or not Plutarch embroidered a good story, and whether or not Stimson's injunction was obeyed, these instances display a moral element at work in public affairs.

Athenian admirals of the fifth century BC and American gentlemen of the twentieth AD are no doubt unrepresentative of the human race in general, but these stories testify that eminent people in positions of responsibility may be aware of and worried by the dilemma between what is right and what is expedient. They also show that expediency usually wins: otherwise the stories would be unremarkable and not worth repeating. The moralist may be depicted as a man of straw who purges his conscience by banging his head against a convenient brick wall or as a holy fool. Forlornly keeping a virtuous flag flying, he may find few people to notice him or his flag; but not entirely. There is a bit of him in nearly all of us. Hermann Goering said that morality stops at the point where the state's interests or its leader's commands override it. The contrary view is that morality stops nowhere in human affairs. For acting on his belief Goering ended up in a court of law.

If moral constraints in public affairs have become less feeble over the ages, how has that come about? Briefly, the answer is: by morality going into partnership with law. The relevance of morality has been promoted by lawyers, people with a fair share of the human awareness of the difference between right and wrong and, in addition, a rather more effective weapon than moral exhortations. Lawyers prescribe precise pains and penalties in this world, not in a problematic next one. Law, even the law of warfare, works because most people most of the time prefer to be on the right side of the law. Thus law and the enforcement of law influence behaviour: especially, one may add, where law is seen to be in concord with morality.

The Greeks and Romans had no legal objection to waging war. The Greeks made no attempt to legislate against war apart from special occasions such as the Olympic Games.[3] In their classical period Greek wars were with few, if memorable, exceptions wars of Greeks against Greeks. The Romans engaged in war on a more uninhibited basis. After the conquest of the Italian peninsula Rome's enemies were barbarians, perennially despised and sometimes feared. Hence a new attitude to war and a sophisticated ambivalence about it which was later copied by Christians. The early Christians, like all persecuted minorities, condemned violence of all kinds and war in particular, but after Constantine I became converted and created the first Christian state Christians became apologists for war and their churches became even zealots. A Christian minority remained pacifist and has kept the pacifist tradition alive for 2,000 years, but the majority preferred to salve its conscience by drawing legal distinctions between wars just and unjust, between wars within Christendom (deplorable) and wars against pagans or heretics (sadly necessary or even pious). In the Middle Ages both the Church and the warrior caste tried to humanise war. Wars were still small. They were waged by small bodies of men under the command of an elite caste which developed into a special corps of professionals. These warriors were ignorant and contemptuous of the law, but evolved nevertheless a code of behaviour of their own, partly out of pride and partly out of self-interest. It has been described as a code of honour and sometimes it was, but codes tend to be less effective in practice than they appear in retrospect and self-regulation by a caste not trained to reflection or noted for its equable temper is a patchy and unreliable affair; and codes – as, for example, the code of chivalry – habitually crystallise when the thing itself is in decline. The Order of

---

3. In ancient times the Games were a time for peace, not for the expression of sublimated national hostilities in the service of profit on television.

the Garter was not created until the Middle Ages and feudal society were nearly over.[4]

Legal codes were less tenuous than codes of honour. They grew out of the Roman belief in the efficiency of law and the Church's search for a legal sanction to underpin the moral sanctions against conduct unbecoming a Christian. St Augustine (354–430), a fairly pugnacious saint, is commonly credited with the beginning of Just War theory. This attempt to square a circle bifurcated into two parts called by lawyers *Jus ad Bellum* and *Jus in Bello*, meaning rules regulating the justified unleashing of a war and rules regulating behaviour in war. The distinction has been maintained into modern times, progressively elaborated and sophisticated and reformulated in the sequences of Hague and Geneva Conventions of the nineteenth and twentieth centuries. For about a thousand years after St Augustine, *Jus ad Bellum* was the more important of the two categories. It was the medieval equivalent of modern Public Order Acts. It sought to establish a tight monopoly of lawful warmaking. A war might be begun by the pope and by a properly qualified prince but not, in the pope's view, by bishops nor, in the prince's view, by inferior feudal lords. *Jus ad Bellum* reduced wars by lesser folk to the category of brawling. Wars were either just or criminal. A war sanctioned by a pope was automatically a Holy War and therefore legitimate; war by a prince was legitimate provided it could show a just cause and a reputable intention.

All other wars were illegal aggression, foreshadowing the charges of aggressive war made in the Nuremberg indictment. In practice, however, in the Middle Ages a war by a prince was unchallenged in law nine times out of ten unless the prince was feeble or an upstart. In due course the right to make war passed from the prince to the absolute monarch and thence to the nation state until in 1945 the right of the state to make war (except in self-defence) was removed from all states which signed or adhered to the UN Charter. This was a big step which the more powerful states took with big reservations and do not in their hearts regard as categorically binding on themselves.

---

4. Codes of behaviour in the upper reaches of modern capitalism are not dissimilar.

More relevant to our present inquiry is *Jus in Bello*, the rules which prescribe what a belligerent may not do even though the state of war legitimises many acts which are illegal in peacetime. It applied less to states than to warriors, to individual behaviour. It had small beginnings: the protection of heralds, ambassadors, clerics and a few other useful or privileged classes of person. It branched out to the prohibition of certain weapons, for example the crossbow which was not to be used against Christians (knights, a conservative class, did not approve of the new-fangled crossbow which their fathers had got on without). There was a measure of protection for civilians, but more often than not civilians who got killed were adjudged to have deserved their fate by getting in the way. They were in the Middle Ages still thin on the ground and apart from the occasional local massacre there was little mass killing of what were later called innocent victims. Christianity both exacerbated the ferocity of war and tried to do the opposite: Christian churches still do.

If *Jus in Bello* originated in a wish to make rules which would make war tidier and more efficient, it was inspired also by a wish to humanise it by banning excesses. In the thirteenth century St Thomas Aquinas (1225–74) applied his systematic mind to the laws of war with a moral purpose. He gave the sanction of the Roman Church (the eastern Orthodox Church was less bothered) to a stricter definition of the rules and stricter limitations to the havoc. He strengthened the link between the moralist and the legist. Subsequently the Renaissance lawyers, notably Hugo Grotius (1587–1645) with his treatise on War and Peace, pursued the subject with their professional mania for precision, cheered on from time to time by churchmen and philosophers. The most important of the doctrines bequeathed by the Middle Ages to later times was the rule that destruction should be proportionate, meaning that the force used and the damage inflicted should be no greater than what was necessary to achieve the war's just purposes. It was all right to squeeze a lemon to get the juice but not to make the pips squeak. Medieval *Jus in Bello* would not have condemned bombing in principal, but it would have condemned the bombing of a particular city either if that bombing served no military purpose or if the bombardment exceeded the requirements of a military purpose or (conceivably but not certainly) if the object were the indiscriminate killing of civilians. You do not need to look long at these definitions to see that they leave the harder questions unanswered.

The nineteenth century began to try to answer them. The laws of war moved from learned treatises and spirited sermons to diplomatic conferences and legal draughtsmen. As the world changed so did war. The industrial revolution, the consolidation of the system of sovereign states, the *levée en masse* made war more destructive of property and lives. War by now meant war between states, each state claiming to be a law unto itself.[5] The first Geneva Convention on the treatment of the wounded, the sick and prisoners of war was adopted in 1864, the forerunner of a series of Geneva Conventions concerned with the victims of war. The Hague Conventions, beginning at the same time and grounded in the broad principle that the infliction of unnecessary suffering is contrary to law, condemned specific weapons (poisons, dumdum bullets) and, more generally, the killing of prisoners and attacks on undefended towns or cities or buildings; they also enjoined respect for religious, historic, artistic and other types of building and limited the rights of belligerents over occupied territory and its inhabitants. These two streams converged to create in the present century the broad field of the laws of warfare, later expanded into the laws of armed conflict. In the same period fresh attempts were made, notably in the Covenant of the League of Nations and the Kellogg-Briand Pact of 1928, to restrict the legitimate recourse to war by stricter conditions for its justification.

As law is made more precise the separate problem of enforcing it becomes more insistent. Law which is not enforced withers. When World War II ended there existed – and there still exists – no international court competent to try war criminals (or criminals of any kind). National courts may do so but for obvious reasons usually do not. At the end of World War I the Treaty of Versailles had obliged Germany to bring war criminals to trial in Germany, but few trials

---

5. The American Civil War was an attempt, on the one side, to turn one sovereign state into two and, on the other, to prevent this. It produced one of the first major pronouncements on the conduct of war in modern conditions: President Abraham Lincoln's General Order No. 100 of 1863 on the Government of Forces in the Field, a set of injunctions and prohibitions devised to humanise war.

took place and those who were condemned found it curiously easy to walk out of the prisons to which they were committed. During the second war, there was some talk of getting neutrals to do the job, but neutrals were few and unwilling. So the winners set up special tribunals at Nuremberg and Tokyo. These were *ad hoc* courts whose competence was defined and limited by the terms of their creation: the Nuremberg tribunal was empowered to prosecute and punish 'Major War Criminals of the European Axis' and in the event tried only Germans. Its jurisdiction was restricted to three categories of crime, of which one was 'War Crimes – namely, violations of the laws and customs of war'. Examples of such crimes included 'destruction not justified by military necessity'. The Nuremberg tribunal therefore was not precluded from considering the legality of bombing in general or in particular cases, but it was precluded from considering accusations of illegal bombing by anybody not in the service of the European Axis. The common complaint that this situation arose because the victorious governments were not disposed to allow their tribunal to try themselves is undeniable. It is also unsurprising. Had there been an established international tribunal with criminal jurisdiction they would have been exceedingly unwilling to see it entertain such proceedings, but they would have had difficulty in preventing it from doing so.

Although the bombing of Dresden lay outside the jurisdiction of the Nuremberg tribunal it did not lie outside the law. It was justiciable, but there was no court to consider it. Mass or area bombing took off from the Casablanca conference of January 1943 and in contravention of earlier declarations of British and American leaders in the highest positions that air raids endangering large numbers of civilians would not take place. Casablanca saw a reversal of these aspirations. In the earlier stages of the war the leaders recoiled from mass bombing partly because, it may be presumed, they regarded it as unacceptably inhumane and partly because they sensed, however vaguely, that it was forbidden, but above all because they hoped that it would not be expedient or, if expedient, could somehow be confined to recognisably military targets with excusable overspill. But by 1943 it was expedient. Therefore they sanctioned it in what amounted to a triumph of expediency over moral and legal rules of behaviour: winning the war came first and this was the way to do it. They thereby gave World War II one of its principal distinguishing features. Whereas civilian victims of World War I were numerically insignificant, in the second war they accounted for half.

Legally there could be no doubt that any operation aimed exclusively against civilians was a war crime. Equally, it would have been difficult to argue that an operation was illegal because a small number of civilians was knowingly put at risk in an otherwise permissible attack. But most military operations against German cities fell between these extremes. They involved military judgements and widespread civilian casualties and when the one was weighed against the other the former prevailed on the plea of military necessity and with few questions asked. To the question who judges military necessity the answer is that military commanders make the judgement in the first place, but a court of law may judge differently later. This is a situation familiar and fundamental in domestic law: every (sane) person acts on his or her assessment of the relevant circumstances, but subject to law. It is one of the functions of international law to extend this principle beyond domestic affairs, to assert that even in wartime an illegal act does not become legal and may not escape retribution because the actor believed it to be legal at the time of the action. That may be a hard rule, but it is part of the price to be paid for the very considerable benefits of living under the rule of law. There will in many cases be mitigating circumstances, but ignorance of the law is not one of them.

If the Dresden raid had come within the purview of a court with competence in the laws of war, a defendant might have pleaded that its purpose was to bring the war to an early end. Four weeks later – on 10 March 1945 – Tokyo was ferociously bombed by 334 Superfortresses in the most devastating and lethal raid of the war. It lasted three hours beginning at midnight and was aimed at the most densely populated part of the city, creating unprecedented firestorms which choked, incinerated and (in the river) boiled 100,000 or perhaps twice as many persons and laid waste a quarter of the city. It did not stop the war. It was followed later in the year by the nuclear bombs on Hiroshima and Nagasaki. The Hiroshima raid could certainly be said to have done much to end the war, but on that assumption the Nagasaki raid did not. Dresden was undefended and it had only minor industrial and military importance. At Nuremberg and at the Tokyo trial commanders-in-chief were tried, convicted and sentenced to long prison terms or to death for war crimes perpetrated on land or sea but not by air. There existed no positive law on aerial bombardment as such, but customary law provided general rules and principles applicable to it: the obstacle was not legal. The tribunal declared and the UN subsequently endorsed the criminality of such breaches of the laws of war and personal accountability for their commission. The bombing of Dresden was not justiciable at Nuremberg, but if it had been it would have been condemned as a crime contrary to long-established law.

The law is not universally obeyed and least of all in time of war. But that is no reason for marginalising law or for failing to make clear what it is.

. . .

III

Where there is law there needs to be law enforcement. Without enforcement law appears pointless and gathers contempt. One of the justifications for the Nuremberg trial was the resolve to enforce the law on war crimes and – more tentatively – the law relating to recourse to war and to humanitarian law. One trial or even a dozen trials may not be enough. In domestic law trials occur every day and by these trials the law is used, defined and affirmed; and the processes of the law run into political toils only exceptionally. The judiciary is kept separate from the executive power as a matter of principle and also because, totalitarian subversion apart, the separation is not difficult to maintain. In the international field, however, trials are few and there is a corresponding urge to seize and make the most of any occasion that turns up. But there are warnings to be sounded, two in particular. The first relates to trials which, for whatever reason, can be brought to court only decades after the event. The second relates to situations in which justice runs counter to non-juridical considerations.

Some crimes are so appalling – and the slaughter of Jews in World War II is an outstanding example – that the pursuit of those criminally responsible seems right and even obligatory regardless of the passage of half a century or more and in spite of the obviously unsafe evidence of identification upon which such cases heavily depend. The layman may forget that prosecutions of this kind entail two distinct judgments: the judgment of a court on the strength of the evidence brought before it and the preliminary judgment of the prosecuting authority on whether the evidence available warrants the launching of a prosecution in the first place. In Britain, where an Act of parliament in 1991 authorised prosecutions for war crimes committed in eastern Europe during World War II, the attorney-general is not, as some might wish him to be, an automaton who is required to forward to court all allegations of such crimes. He is a law enforcement officer whose duty it is to distinguish allegations from evidence and to persuade himself that in instituting a prosecution he will not be wasting the time of the court by submitting allegations insufficiently backed by reliable evidence. The passage of time is one of the weightiest of the relevant considerations. Time does not wipe out criminal liability, but it may wipe out the evidence.[6] There is no legal time limit for bringing criminal proceedings (there are such limits to civil cases) and a person accused of a crime may not plead immunity from prosecution simply because his accusers have not caught up with him more promptly. But the prosecutor himself must consider whether time and its impact on human memory may not have reduced the likelihood of a conviction so far that to press for one will either be a waste of time (in the sense that the prosecution has little chance of succeeding) or, more seriously, will court a miscarriage of justice. Not only are memories fallible; the longer they fester the more likely are they to be coloured by vengefulness. To bring to court with more zest than rigour a sequence of poorly supported cases brings the law into contempt, particularly where national or sectarian interests may be inferred. Many people were outraged by the Russian insistence on keeping Rudolf Hess in prison after he was a feeble old man, but at least he was accused, tried and sentenced within a few years of his crimes. Justice tinged with vengefulness may still be justice

6. In *Polykhoritch* v. *The Commonwealth* in Australia in 1993, half a century after the events adduced, the accused was acquitted largely on grounds of suspect identification.

but it is an unclean justice which does the cause of justice more harm than good.[7]

The second warning against expecting too much of international criminal law may be tested against the war in Bosnia which developed from 1991 out of the disintegration of the Yugoslav federation. It did so with a viciousness and depravity which appalled Europeans as deeply as the atrocities of World War II and created a demand for the condign punishment of criminals on the analogy of Nuremberg. In 1993 the Security Council established an *ad hoc* tribunal to consider and try allegations of certain kinds of crime committed after 1991 in the former Yugoslavia, and in the following year the International Law Commission submitted to the General Assembly a draft statute for a permanent court. This draft contained detailed provisions concerning the court's jurisdiction, its constitution, the right to initiate prosecutions, safeguards for a fair trial, sentences, appeals and so on, but the crux of the matter is to arrive at a balance between what is legally sound and judicially effective and, on the other hand, also politically acceptable. In theory it is within the competence of any number of states, in the joint exercise of their several sovereignties, to create a court with international jurisdiction. They may do so by an international treaty or convention which would bind them but not other states. In practice, however, no court will command attention if its creators are few or insignificant.

That justice required the institution of criminal proceedings against suspect war criminals in Bosnia was undeniable, but the analogy with Nuremberg was imperfect because there were in the Bosnian case two imperatives, not one. The one was justice and the other was peace and they conflicted with one another. In 1946 there was peace in Europe, but in Bosnia in the 1990s there was not and the restoration of peace seemed to many to be the overriding need not only for the men, women and children of Bosnia but also for people in a much wider zone to which the fighting might quickly spread. The only attainable peace was peace by negotiation; peace by the total surrender of one or more of the belligerents was impossible. Diplomats from a number

7. The old Courts of Equity in England had a maxim which said that he who comes to Equity must come with clean hands.

of countries laboured to secure such a peace in circumstances which defeated them for years. Some of those with whom they negotiated were suspect, even indicted, war criminals. The proposal to prosecute these men was an additional impediment to pacification since men do not come to the negotiating table if on their appearance they may be arrested and condemned to long years in prison (in this particular case the death penalty had been ruled out).

The backgrounds of Nuremberg and Bosnia were profoundly different and the former was the more unusual, for it included the total defeat and unconditional surrender of one of the belligerents, a rare occurrence. The Nuremberg tribunal handled great issues, not perfectly but nevertheless well. But its achievements cannot be easily or frequently repeated and judicial proceedings have not become a regular part of the mechanisms for the extension of the rule of law in international affairs, least of all in relation to the laws of warfare. It is better not to pretend that they have. No permanent international criminal court has been created nor, between 1946 and 1993, has any *ad hoc* court, in spite of the fact that an international criminal court would have had plenty of business if it had existed.

Outbursts of furious criminality – as in Bosnia, Rwanda and elsewhere or, less widely publicised, criminal conduct by governments which torture dissident or merely tiresome citizens – kindle demands for the creation of a permanent criminal court. The mere existence of such a court would facilitate the arraignment of suspects and so perhaps restrain illegal brutality. A permanent court has more authority and accessibility than an *ad hoc* court. When at the end of World War II the UN Charter was being drafted and the role of the International Court of Justice at The Hague was being reviewed, an international criminal court might have been established, but paradoxically the Nuremberg and Tokyo proceedings thwarted that possibility since it seemed sensible to await the outcome of those trials and the codification of the law in the light of their final judgments. In 1948 the UN General Assembly asked the International Law Commission to study the feasibility of an international criminal court, but the issue was consigned to limbo by the Cold War. It was revived with the end of the Cold War and the proliferation of fresh atrocities in various parts of the world, but the old obstacles were still there. Just as an effective national judiciary is a threat to malefactors, so an effective international judiciary is regarded as a threat by governments which might be arraigned before it and are intent on preserving their sovereign right to be judged in their own causes. These governments may be willing to try, in their own courts and by their own domestic law, persons accused of international crimes, but they baulk at conceding jurisdiction over their own nationals to any other court and view with horror any suggestion that their own leaders might be so arraigned.[8] At the present time any proposal to create an international criminal court would certainly be vetoed in the Security Council, probably by all five of its veto-holding members. Only a narrower body – perhaps the European Union – might make the venture in the foreseeable future, but the hard fact is that law, although some sort of cousin to morality, is no better than distant and quarrelsome kin with politics and diplomacy.

Nothing said or done at Nuremberg made future Dresdens impossible, but that trial did make them somewhat more difficult: first, by clarifying the legal arguments about mass aerial bombardment and about the rule of proportionality; and, secondly, by asserting personal individual accountability for war crimes, even if committed in the name of and with the authority of the state. On the other hand, the problem of enforcing law in these matters has been rendered no easier either at Nuremberg or since that trial took place fifty years ago. The tribunals established in 1993 and 1994 by the Security Council to hear cases arising from atrocities in Yugoslavia and Rwanda avoided some of Nuremberg's blemishes: they were without the stigma of 'victors' justice', their jurisdiction embraced crimes against humanity whether committed in connection with war or not, and they bypassed the argument whether the conflicts in Bosnia and Rwanda were international or civil wars. But they were severely hampered by lack of evidence, particularly documentary evidence,

8. The trial in the United States of Lt. Calley for crimes in and around My Lai in Vietnam was such a trial. It was not a trial under international law or before an international court. In the later case of *Filartiga* the Supreme Court of the United States affirmed the right of domestic American courts to try foreign nationals accused of certain categories of crime against international law committed outside the United States.

and the difficulties of combining the play of politics with the demands of justice were exemplified by what was in effect an American refusal to allow the arrest of Radovan Karadzic or Radko Mladic on warrants duly issued by a UN chief prosecutor and easily executable by an international force on the spot.

There is, in conclusion, a novel development worth noting. The end of *apartheid* and white minority rule in South Africa was in no conventional sense the end of a war but it marked the collapse of a regime which had encouraged and itself practised gross inhumanities and illegalities and it raised demands for justice and retribution. Court proceedings, however, have satisfied neither legists nor the victims of past crimes and irregularities. In parallel with these legal proceedings a Truth and Reconciliation Commission was created not so much to settle old scores as to clear the air. Such a Commission is no substitute for the enforcement of law but it may be a useful supplement among attempts to salve a bitterly riven society.

Chapter 4

WINSTON CHURCHILL: STATESMAN

. . .

I

Winston Churchill lived for ninety years. World War II lasted for less than six. He won enduring fame in a short passage in a long life. His career and his character were exceptionally and intriguingly full of paradox. More than any of his contemporaries he determined the set of Europe's history at the most critical moment of the twentieth century by his refusal to countenance peace with Germany in 1940 or 1941. He thereby ensured the defeat of Germany by the Soviet Union and the United States of America and the denial of German domination of the continent of Europe.

His career: in 1939 it seemed to be finished, not merely because he was sixty-five years old, but because by and large he was a failure. Although he had held half a dozen of the principal great offices of state he had held none for ten years and was not expected ever to hold another. Franklin D. Roosevelt by contrast had been president of the United States for the past seven years and Stalin had wielded power continuously for more than twice as long. Beside them Churchill was a has-been. He had few political friends and did not seek to build a rogue political party: he was a rogue politician without a party. He was chiefly remarked for championing lost or dubious causes: the Dardanelles strategy in World War I; the return to the Gold Standard in 1925 at a crippling overvaluation; Edward VIII; the defence of the Raj, the whole Raj and nothing but the Raj. These eccentricities were the more damaging since he had no compelling reason to be loyal to Edward VIII, he knew little about India and as little about economics, and the Gallipoli expedition was not so much a bad idea as a sloppily executed one. The overall impression was misplaced impulsiveness or insufficient application. His advocacy of rearmament in the 1930s won some sympathy, most of it delayed, but Conservatives vastly preferred the reassuring complacency of Baldwin or even the brooding efficiency of Neville Chamberlain. On the Left his pre-World War I credentials as a reforming minister and ally of Lloyd George were overlaid by his pugnacity against strikes by the working classes in and after that war: he seemed a wayward politician who had come to rest irrevocably on the Right.

He was not a party man. He might have been termed a maverick if that word were not normally associated with left-wing, not right-wing misfits. He was moved by ideas, not by programmes. What he savoured in politics was high themes, debate, the hustings, the bending of minds; not committees, shaping Acts of parliaments or the whipping of votes. He had an image of himself as a statesman, a superior person whose superiority is directed to the public service and who maintains a certain independence from the herdlike parties which, with the growth of the franchise, had supplanted the political coteries of an earlier age. This approach to public life may be dubbed independence (good) or volatility (bad) and in Churchill's case it won him more bad marks than good, at any rate among politicians in peacetime. His father, Lord Randolph Churchill, was a Tory grandee, party leader, secretary of state for India and chancellor of the exchequer: also a trenchant speaker, uncomfortable colleague and unstable failure. He called himself a Democrat. His more famous son exemplified many of these traits at one stage or another of a much longer career. Beginning as a Conservative he was soon a Liberal. He entered the House of Commons as a Conservative in 1900 at the age of twenty-five, got office as a Liberal in 1905 and was in the cabinet in 1908 where he became a political ally and friend of Lloyd George on the left of the Liberal Party. He had a strong sense of fairness – a hunch that politics was a blend of morality and expediency – which placed him in that section of the aristocracy which thought that the workers and the poor should have a better deal, though not a better place in the social order. They should on the contrary know their place and keep to it and when they did not – when, for example, they went on strike – he was among their severest opponents. What made him temporarily a Liberal or at least a member of the Liberal Party was his belief that the existing order could and should be improved, not that it should be radically changed as Lloyd George believed. He remained a Liberal until after World War I when he was lured back by Baldwin into a Conservative government as chancellor of the exchequer. He resigned – over India – seven years later. Essentially he was a wandering Whig who joined the Conservatives later than most Whigs, but by this time few people knew what a Whig was.

In character Churchill was a romantic with an imaginative and restless mind, powerful emotions and uncommon resoluteness: not a comfortable make-up. In childhood he was neglected by his parents and hurt by their neglect. They failed to disguise their preference for their many social and political activities. He was neither physically distinguished nor intellectually brilliant and his school years were lustreless, but he possessed a sharp and well cultivated intelligence. He read much, the grind along with the floss, and was quick at seizing on the central point in an argument or a tale. He was not cumbered, as cleverer men are apt to be, by the ability to see every side of a question and the compulsion to give equal weight to every argument. He was undevious, generous, but capable of some ruthlessness; exuberant but subject to attacks of deep depression; he possessed that all but indispensable element in good judgement – a sense of humour; he was not afraid of responsibility, but not immune from doubt in the exercise of it; he was a good listener. Party politics apart he was conservative. He preferred to contemplate the past rather than the future. He knew a great deal more than most politicians about his country's past and thought well of it – or perhaps he best remembered what best he liked. Of the future he was wary because it held threats to the past which he venerated. He believed that the more firmly the future was attached to the past the more likely was it to work. His idealism was backward-looking, but with the reservation that what he sought in the past was moral precepts by which to guide the present and mould the future. He was an educated man – more self-educated than the general run of his time and class – in an

age when higher education was still essentially literary, philo-
sophical and classical rather than scientifically adventurous.

He was born into the ruling class, the grandson of a duke.
Although his paternal line had achieved little since the first
Duke of Marlborough, that duke had been one of the greatest military men in English history, had commanded international armies, fashioned international politics and saved
Europe from Louis XIV in spite of the obstructiveness of
mean-spirited allies (the duke's less attractive qualities, which
were many and pronounced, did not dim his glory in his
descendant's eyes). He knew little about the lower classes.
He neither disliked nor admired them, but, unlike more
middle-class Conservatives, he did not fear them and when
called by circumstances to lead he did so in regal mode and
with enormous acclaim. He spoke and wrote splendidly.
He had the strengths and weaknesses of a proud narrow
patriotism which served to focus his foreign and imperial
attitudes which were wholeheartedly Anglocentric. He had
comparatively little understanding of foreign places: India
enthralled him because the English had done great things
there, Europe engaged him because Europeans had historically affected the fortunes of Britain and might do so again,
Russia disturbed him because – again historically – it had
trespassed too close to British India. Russia also repelled
him because it had tried to tear up its past by the brutal
destruction of the old order; its communism affronted his
profound attachment to traditions which the tsar, however
personally inadequate, embodied. Where liberty and tradition were at odds, caution and temperament inclined him
to the latter. He disliked foreign upstarts, but his dislike
only expanded into hostility when the upstart threatened to
do damage to British interests. He at first approved of Mussolini, but his approval turned to disparagement when the
Duce became too big for his boots and developed pretensions to challenge Britain's dominance of the Mediterranean.
Of Franco, who made no such cheeky claims to Gibraltar,
he never spoke ill until the Generalissimo had won his war.
Hitler was different. Churchill was profoundly and genuinely
appalled by the Nazis's excesses, but he was no less alarmed
by the resurgence of German power. Hitler's renewal of
Germany's hegemonial aggressiveness was as fearful as his
barbarism. Churchill did not hold Germans to be worse

than other people, but he specially feared German power in Europe. Nazism was a spur to his anti-Germanism and the source of much of his most effective oratory.

Churchill had a certain pugnacity which derived from the directness of his manner, his fondness for the bulldog image, his awareness of the power of his oratory and his isolation – personal isolation in prewar politics, national isolation in the first war years. World War II has been described as his great opportunity, but if this judgement implies that war was his natural milieu it is superficial. He did not crave war, but he did crave dramas and war supplied drama. His direct experience of war was unusually varied. In his earlier years he had been a professional soldier and, like a number of aristocratic sprigs in doubt about what to do in life, had served in odd places from Cuba to Sudan to the North West Frontier of India where his lively eye had picked up abiding impressions: his eye taught him as much as his reason in his formative years and his eye in harness with his perseverance made him a tolerably adept amateur painter. He was a well-liked and well-regarded officer and he became the chronicler of colonial wars in which he had played a part as officer of journalist. He also served on the western front in World War I. The alternation of trench warfare and mass slaughter in that war dismayed him. He wrote about wars with relish, but neither insensitively nor vindictively. They evoked some of the most stirring prose in his life (in four volumes) of his great ancestor Marlborough and his best book – *The World Crisis* – is a book about himself on the stage of war. He never wrote a book about a soldier who was not a relative or himself. He talked about writing about Napoleon but did not do so. He chose rather to write about England and the English-speaking peoples (plural) and he thought of himself as, like Chatham, a Great Commoner rather than a Great Captain. He refused to become the twentieth century's only new (non-royal) duke. He liked dressing up but the uniforms he favoured were distinctly unmilitary. He saw war for what it was: a failure to secure political ends by other means, and an absurdity as well as a calamity. Although at the war's end he became a prophet and pillar of the Cold War, he never ceased to brood over how to stop it by the forces of reason and talk, if not with Stalin then with somebody else when the pickled communist dictator died.

Churchill was a man of extraordinary stamina and activity. The one thing which devastated him was having nothing to do, having time on his hands. The myths which nourished his imagination and sustained him in hard times were historical, not religious. Religion was one of the many subjects which did not attract him. In extreme old age, when time and infirmity had forced him out of public life, he sank gradually into silent misery in which he communed not with his Maker about his eternal life to come, but with himself alone about his place in history and his service to his country: about, we may suppose, those six years at war.

. . .

II

Churchill's role in World War II began with peripheral incompetence, central disaster and enforced waiting: the bungled campaign in Norway, the collapse of France and waiting for the Americans. These experiences took up nearly half the war.

Within a week of the outbreak of war this highly untypical man in the political wilderness was first lord of the admiralty and within eight months prime minister and minister of defence, i.e. war supremo. The first of these two moves was occasioned by Hitler's invasion of Poland, the second by Hitler's invasion of Norway. Churchill was conscripted to stop Hitler. He did not do that, but without him those who did would not have done. He had an *idée fixe*: that the survival of Hitler and the Nazis was incompatible with British interests and with European civilisation.

He had also fixed ideas about how to run the war. He had been in, and had been thrown out of, the cabinet in World War I. He was out of it when Lloyd George was prime minister: Lloyd George was prime minister for less than half the first war, Churchill for almost all of the second. He was not unembarrassed by domestic politics but he suffered nothing like the tribulations which beset Lloyd George and, before him, Asquith. He became leader of the Conservative Party on Chamberlain's death at the end of 1940, but more on account of the feebleness of the party's leadership than its love for him. His coalition partners, Labour and Liberal, were of exemplary loyalty, even if non-party colleagues – notably

Beaverbrook – were not. There was no Lloyd George to his Asquith. Above all Churchill quickly gained a popularity outside government which made him all but irremovable. He was trusted – a rare homage and incalculably important in a democracy at war.

Disasters such as the loss of Singapore and Tobruk deeply distressed him but did not seriously threaten his position which he strengthened from the start by concentrating on the war and leaving most other things most of the time to others. By making himself minister of defence as well as prime minister he took the conduct of the war into his own hands with the chiefs of staff as an inner council (although not so called) and he left the cabinet to look after home affairs. In effect he downgraded the cabinet which, although called the war cabinet, was not allowed to have much to do with the war. The chiefs of staff he cowed. Revolts against his way of handling things were few and futile. His machinery of government was strong and he controlled those matters which he wanted to control, restrained less by ministers than by his respect for the democratic system and parliament. Parliament trusted him most of the time and was swayed by him when it had doubts. Broadly speaking, he took responsibility for conducting and winning the war in its two aspects of high diplomacy and grand strategy. Here was boldness. After their first meeting de Gaulle summed him up: *Il est fait pour les tâches grandioses.*

The Norwegian adventure of April 1940 had its origins in an Anglo-French plan to seize, in defiance of Norwegian neutrality, the port of Narvik which was ice-free throughout the year and the main outlet for Sweden's iron ore to Germany. The British and French planned to use the Russo-Finnish war as cover for their action. When this war ended the plan was first abandoned and then revived and recast as an operation to mine the territorial waters of the Narvik approaches and so force German vessels into international waters where they would be captured by British warships. This operation coincided with an utterly unsuspected German operation to occupy Norway with sea, air and land forces. The allied operation was a bumbling concatenation of shifting aims, shifting tactics and muddled chains of command and when it resulted in the loss of 4–5,000 men and an aircraft carrier there was uproar in Britain.

Chamberlain's majority in the House of Commons withered to a point where some of his party were able to demand a remodelling of the government. The Labour and Liberal leaders refused to serve in a coalition under him, Halifax was outmanoeuvred and Churchill took Chamberlain's place. Churchill had contributed more than a little to the Norwegian fiasco, but this episode was pushed into the background by the German invasion of the Low Countries and France which occurred on the day on which he became prime minister. (Both Germans and French ignored the Maginot Line which was supposed to demarcate the war and protect France.)

Churchill's first task as prime minister was to keep the Anglo-French alliance alive and fighting. In this he failed. It is inconceivable that anybody else could have succeeded. The Germans beat the French into surrender and there was no chance that a French government would carry on the war from overseas. Any French politicians who declared themselves a government operating temporarily from Africa would have been ignored by the Germans and the French in France too. France was in the power of Germany and of whomever the Germans chose to delegate power to. The smash was complete – except for one thing, the French fleet.

The size and quality of the French fleet being what they were, the prospect of it falling into German hands and being deployed at sea in support of Germany's commerce raiders and U-boats threw Churchill into something like panic. Determined to prevent the unconditional surrender of the fleet, he allowed his determination to override the practical necessities. While it can validly be said that he was right to take no chances, it is also clear in retrospect that he need not have issued the orders which he did issue and which, by killing over a thousand Frenchmen, did more lasting damage to Anglo-French relations than Englishmen have been prepared to acknowledge.

The French fleet was dispersed in French and North African ports. Churchill pressed the French to insist in their armistice negotiations with the Germans on terms which would prevent any of the ships being used to Britain's detriment so long as Britain remained at war. The commander-in-chief of the French navy, Admiral Jean Darlan, was anti-German and anti-British and distrusted by both, although more on account of his manner than any valid disbelief in his integrity: he was difficult, even disagreeable, but not dishonourable. He told Churchill early in June that the French fleet would never be surrendered to the Germans and, if in danger, would sail on his orders to British ports. Churchill was not reassured. Before the conclusion of the Franco-German armistice on 24 June Pétain, who had succeeded Reynaud as prime minister, told the British ambassador that although he would not order the fleet to British ports he would order it to scuttle rather than surrender to the Germans. This determination was confirmed by the French cabinet and on separate occasions by Darlan once more, by the French foreign minister Paul Baudoin (to Churchill personally) and by President Albert Lebrun. Churchill was still apprehensive, talked about using force to secure or sink the fleet, but was dissuaded by his cabinet colleagues and naval advisers. The Franco-German armistice turned out to be surprisingly lenient in regard to the fleet.

True to their word the French put the fate of the fleet at the top of their agenda for armistice discussions. Their negotiators were instructed to insist that their refusal to surrender it on terms which would leave it available for use against Britain was not negotiable. Leaving Tours, where the French government was temporarily perched in its flight from Paris to Bordeaux, they returned to Paris on their way to Rethonde, near Compiègne, where they had the disagreeable experience of finding themselves face to face with Hitler and an array of German leaders in the very carriage in which the armistice of November 1918 had been signed and which since that date had been on show in the Invalides in Paris. After an initial session Hitler and others left and the business was conducted by the Wehrmacht chiefs, Keitel and Jodl. The document presented by the Germans provided that all French vessels should return to their peacetime home ports in France, but that the Germans would undertake in the subsequent peace treaty not to use them or lay claim to them. The French delegates tried to get this article modified by substituting North African for French ports, but failed and felt that nevertheless they did discharge their obligations to Britain. The article was not immediately disclosed to the British who continued to fear the worst.

In the event a few of the vessels in French Atlantic ports were scuttled, but the greater number, including the battleship *Jean Bart* at St Nazaire, sailed to Africa. At Alexandria the French and British admirals reached an amicable agreement which obviated all the more repugnant outcomes; the French made no attempt to leave port or to scuttle and the British made no attempt to board French ships. All were disarmed and their complement repatriated to France with the exception of skeleton crews. The trouble was in Algeria where the bulk of the fleet was based at Mers el-Kebir. Churchill was convinced that these ships, which included the battleships *Strasbourg* and *Dunquerque,* were safe only in British hands or at the bottom of the sea. He despatched Admiral James Somerville with an imposing force from Gibraltar to demand of Admiral Gensoul at Mers el-Kebir that he scuttle or surrender to the British. Somerville meanwhile had given Gensoul a wider choice: to continue the war alongside the British, to sail to British ports or the United States or the Caribbean, or to scuttle with the ultimate sanction that in default of any of these solutions his ships would be engaged and destroyed. Gensoul, who was already disarming his ships, reported the terms of this ultimatum to Darlan at Vichy, but without mentioning two of the options given him: that of sailing to the Americas and that of scuttling. Gensoul also showed Somerville's emissary, whom he had received on his flagship, Darlan's order to him to sail to the Americas if the Germans showed signs of trying to seize his ships. This was welcome news to Somerville who hoped that a violent encounter was thereby avoided, but Churchill had learned from intercepted traffic that the French ships at Oran and Toulon had been ordered to Mers el-Kebir, assumed that they were going to reinforce Gensoul and instructed Somerville to enforce his ultimatum before nightfall that day. Somerville carried out his orders. In the course of a quarter of an hour on 3 July (followed by an air attack two days later) *Strasbourg* and a number of lesser vessels escaped to France, *Dunquerque* ran aground attempting to escape, the rest were sunk and nearly 1,300 French sailors were killed or drowned. This deplorable affair has been reduced in many English accounts to the level of a lamentable necessity. It had not seemed like that to the French. Its immediate consequence included the rupture of diplomatic relations (presumably not far away in any event) and the failure of the great majority of French servicemen in Britain to join de Gaulle instead of returning to France. (There were about 110,000 of these servicemen, stranded in Britain after being rescued from Norway or Dunkirk. Some 2,000 joined de Gaulle. It is difficult to tell how many of the others chose not to because of the events at Mers el-Kebir, how many because they had never heard of this still unknown junior general.) More lastingly the action at Mers el-Kebir by France's ally in the hour of France's bitter humiliation was not forgotten or forgiven for many years to come. In a broadcast from London de Gaulle expressed his anger, but added that he would rather see French ships beneath the waves than in use by the Germans against the British.

In retrospect some of the blame may be ascribed to poor communications between Gensoul and Vichy and Somerville and London, but the abiding question is how far the French fleet, or a substantial part of it, in German hands could have damaged Britain. To judge by their own actions the Germans did not regard it as a major new weapon, but Churchill judged otherwise. In doing so he discounted two considerable factors: the almost certain refusal of a very large part of the French navy to obey orders to fight against Britain and the very great difficulty which Admiral Raeder would have faced in finding German crews to man French ships.

Preventing the Germans from getting hold of the French fleet was Churchill's most urgent problem in the summer of 1940. It was mismanaged. That is not to say that it could easily have been better managed in those grim days, but hindsight, which is an honourable tool, must record an adverse verdict. The consequences went deeper in France than the British cared to imagine. There was at the same time a less urgent but more basic problem: whether with France knocked out Britain too should concede victory to Hitler or at least probe the terms on which peace might be made. That Hitler was willing to talk peace was clear enough and indeed obvious *a priori* since he had no reason not to.

Even before the French collapsed, the end of Dutch and Belgian resistance, the eviction of all British forces from the continent and gathering doubts about the French capacity or will to fight on had obliged British leaders to ask themselves whether the war was not over. There was in the cabinet a majority for at least taking soundings and the foreign secretary Lord Halifax went so far as to declare that he would resign if this was not done (he soon withdrew his threat). Churchill adamantly opposed this course and prevailed by rallying non-cabinet ministers, but the French collapse intensified the tussle which many, including Halifax and his deputy R.A. Butler, styled bravado versus commonsense. Churchill's main weapons were his intransigence and his inner conviction. He was convinced that the war must be won, not abandoned, and that it was a war against German power and not just against a Hitlerite faction or gang. He was deaf to those who were willing to regard Goering, for example, as an acceptable alternative to Hitler – less uncouth, less maniacal, a man with whom one could do business (as Chamberlain had believed Hitler to be). For Churchill the war was about German domination of Europe, the question at the root of World War I and left unsolved at the end of that conflict. If and so far as he formulated war aims, his aim was to destroy the Nazis as a precondition for restoring a balance of power in Europe: once war had been begun there was no sense in ending it without a decisive German defeat. For that overriding purpose Britain had gone to war and must risk all else. How much was risked is clearer after the event than it was to Churchill or anybody else at the time. It included the defeat of Britain by Germany, the extrusion of Britain from Europe and the end of the British empire. Part of the price, the last part, was eventually paid and the cost of persevering with the original resolve in the face of the daunting facts of 1940 was four more years of war, millions of dead, grievous destruction at home and loss of assets overseas. The difference between Britain and France in the summer of 1940 was that Britain had a choice and France had not. In that respect the French position was the simpler. Britain's was the harder precisely because it had a choice. Few in Europe had it: only the Vatican and the Soviet Union which chose to do a deal and Britain which refused to. This was a gamble since Churchill could not foresee the outcome, but he could see that he must gamble because what was at stake was Hitler's bid to dominate all continental Europe and perhaps in his more visionary moments the world. When the question of peace arose again a year later the context had changed but the central issue had not. Hitler, on the verge of his biggest military adventure, his invasion of the Soviet Union, might be more disposed to make peace with Britain than he had been in 1940, but Britain's withdrawal from the war would have ensured German (or possibly Soviet) domination of the continent and those who, in 1940 and 1941, were prepared to consider a peace with this outcome did not understand what the war was about. Those who echo their views fifty years later are similarly benighted.

．　．　．

III

Churchill never believed that Britain could defeat Germany unaided. In British history, which he had studied, Britain fought colonial wars on its own but grander wars only with allies. Allies were always a problem, but they were necessary. They had to be wooed – even, in the past, paid – and their views had to be accommodated. When Churchill became prime minister France, Belgium and the Netherlands were allies, but they were soon effaced. Then for a year Britain had no ally. It acquired two by adventitious circumstances: the Soviet Union when Hitler invaded it in June 1941, and the United States when Hitler declared war on it in December after the Japanese attack on Pearl Harbor.[1] Hitler therefore presented Churchill with the allies with whom he proceeded to victory, but also with his paramount problem

---

1. This was not purely reckless or thoughtless folly but it was a bad miscalculation. In a world war every combatant is exposed to the risks of fighting on two fronts. Hitler was exploiting this situation. In 1941 he had as yet no way of coming to grips with the United States but Japan had and did, whereupon Hitler swiftly joined the aggressor – three days after Pearl Harbor. But the United States weathered the Japanese storm and proved itself capable of fighting and winning on two fronts. Throughout the rest of the war there were tussles over the distribution of the American effort between two fronts but a rapidly dwindling prospect of American defeat on either. Although the Japanese fleet was a far greater addition to the German cause than the French could have been, the creation of an active German-Japanese alliance disappointed Hitler's hopes because Japan refused, in spite of persistent German pressure, to match the German declaration of war against the United States by declaring war on the Soviet Union.

in the second half of the war – the problem of adapting
or deflecting their wishes and urging his on them. Before
that critical moment the ground theme of Churchill's war
was waiting for the Americans.[2]

Having allies was a vast relief, but the gains were slow in
coming. The Americans did not sail east until the end of
1942 when they made for Africa, not Europe. The Russians,
more of a drain than a gain for a year or more, thwarted
the German invasion of 1941, but did not inflict their searing defeats on the German armies until 1943 (Stalingrad,
Kursk). Britain remained constrained (saved from invasion
by the Battle of Britain), but still threatened by the U-boats
and unable to do more against Germany than nibble at
occupied Europe by blockade, air raids and instigations to
guerrilla warfare stretching German power but not coming
directly to grips with it. The exception was the Mediterranean and North Africa, where operations were continuous
from 1940 to the final surrender in 1945.

The Battle of Britain (wholly) and the Battle of the Atlantic (largely) were British battles. The battle for the Mediterranean and around its shores – North Africa, Greece, Syria
– began as a British battle, expanded into combined British
and Commonwealth campaigns and halfway through the
war became progressively a theatre where the Americans
dominated but took some care to allow the British roughly
equal status in recognition of their earlier achievements and
on condition that Americans set the geographical limits
for active operations. From the winter of 1942–43 awkward
questions arose of shared commands and flustered emotions
against a background of: where do we go from here? Churchill was wedded to the Mediterranean as a principal war theatre because it included a glorious victory (El Alamein) and
because it gratified his personal instinct for making war by
darting about all around enemy lines and, when faced with
a choice between one operation and another, choosing to
do both. He was engaged in the Mediterranean by his sense

2. So it was in World War I after 1916. The French waited for the Americans to enter the line on the western front in 1918. In London Lloyd
   George and Robertson, at loggerheads on practically everything, were
   divided. The prime minister was in favour of waiting, the chief of the
   imperial general staff in favour of another big show – which turned
   out to be Passchendaele.

of history and his sense of empire. Malta was a word that stirred him deeply and, more seriously, he was more alive than most people to the continuity linking the Mediterranean with the Middle East. From 1940 to 1944 the Mediterranean was the one area where the British could get to grips with an enemy (apart from Ethiopia which was an extension of the war against Italy) and after 1942 it remained very much a British affair, however significant the Commonwealth and American – and French – contributions. But Churchill did not regard it as an alternative to a major onslaught on Germany by way of northern France. He saw it as a going concern to be got on with.

The war in North Africa began with the British campaign against the Italians in the winter of 1940–41 devised by Wavell and endorsed by Churchill. Wavell's forces advanced rapidly to Benghazi. Wavell wanted to go on to Tripoli, but Churchill interposed a veto. The problem of Greece arose: whether or not to send forces from Africa to help the Greeks against the Italians who had invaded Greece through Albania and against the Germans who were threatening to invade it to get their Italian allies out of trouble. Churchill could not make up his mind, then acquiesced. Wavell too was in two minds. No decision was taken until February 1941 when forces withdrawn from Wavell's North African operations were despatched to Greece on the basis of plans discussed between British and Greek chiefs of staff (Dill and Papagos) and interpreted by them in different ways: the first link in a chain of disasters. At the same time German forces arrived in North Africa with one of Hitler's favourite generals, Erwin Rommel. Churchill could have backed out of the Greek commitment but he did not like to let Papagos down and gave too much weight to over-optimistic advice from both Dill and Wavell. At the end of March an anti-German coup in Belgrade drew Hitler too into the Balkans. A few days later a coup in Baghdad established an anti-British regime in Iraq. Hitler was now set to succour the Italians in Greece as well as North Africa and was offering to send arms to the new government in Iraq which, in the British view of things, was half way to India. The Germans overran Greece in next to no time in April and occupied Crete at the beginning of May. Wavell's weakened forces were defeated in North Africa, a counter-attack in June failed (Rommel had better equipment and supplies) and Wavell was sacked. All this was the prelude to Act One.

Act One witnessed the tug-of-war in the North African deserts and coastlines which was eventually won at El Alamein in October 1942, followed by the trek of the British and Commonwealth forces westward to join hands with the Americans and British who landed in Morocco and Algeria in November. Between these two forces lay Tunisia. Most of Hitler's advisers counselled him to withdraw Rommel's German and Italian forces from Tunisia, but Kesselring, in Rome, took the opposite view and urged Hitler to reinforce them.[3] Hitler preferred Kesselring's advice and took it and the Axis kept a foothold in Africa until May 1943 thanks to this decision, to the leisurely progress of the allied forces from the east, initial mistakes in the west and French obstructiveness to the Anglo-Americans in Tunisia. The outcome was a foreseeable conclusion but the timing went astray so that when Churchill and Roosevelt met at Casablanca in January to decide what to do next – to write a script for Act Two – their basic assumptions were wrong. Churchill assumed that the campaigns in train would be over in a month or so, that the Mediterranean was now an allied sea and that Normandy would be invaded that year. He wanted more operations in the Mediterranean as well. But between him and Roosevelt there was here no true meeting of minds. Whereas Churchill, like many Englishmen, felt at home in the Mediterranean, few Americans felt that way. For Roosevelt and his advisers, civilian and military, the Mediterranean was a sideshow undertaken before the United States came into the war and now due for decommissioning. As things turned out there were more Mediterranean operations in 1943 and beyond, but no invasion of Normandy until 1944. The Casablanca programme whittled itself away for two main reasons: the failure to secure the surrender of the German-Italian armies in Tunisia until May 1943 and the creeping difficulties of adjusting plans adopted by allies who met face

3. Reading Kesselring's intercepted signals was one of the more fascinating plums for those working on Ultra at Bletchley Park. Kesselring's persuasiveness was, however, not obviously sound since, although it kept the German-Italian armies in Africa for several extra months, it also weakened the German forces at and around Stalingrad, particularly air forces.

to face only once in a while. Although American and British leaders were in permanent and regular contact with one another, their personal encounters were necessarily sparse and their decisions were at the mercy of the twists of events and non-events. There was also a pervasive uncertainty about the main purpose of an invasion of Italy. Churchill famously referred to the Mediterranean in general and Italy in particular as the soft underbelly of the Axis. This fruity phrase, designed to hearten the multitude rather than sharpen the brains of staff officers, could mean either that the Italians were a push-over or that Germany was specially vulnerable from Italy. In the first case, which cast the Italians as the prime target, a relatively modest force might be expected to knock Italy out of the war in a relatively short time. But if the prime purposes of an invasion of Italy was to defeat the Germans (and the Italians only incidentally) then larger forces would have to be employed and bolder strategies too: there was the possibility that an Italian collapse would entail a German withdrawal and the opening of a pincer front against Germany itself, but planners had to assume the contrary and everything which they knew about Hitler and Kesselring pointed to a second resolve to reinforce and hold German positions in Italy as far south as possible: Kesselring argued strongly against a retreat to Tuscany. Strategically Italy was part of the German war zone regardless of its political complexion. In the event the Italian campaigns were turned by Hitler into a major and prolonged confrontation, the underbelly was not soft and the allies' victories were no more than marginal. They entered Rome only one day before the landings in Normandy and eighteen months after the date set by the allied command in the Mediterranean.

Act Two therefore was stitched together on the (slow) trot. It was hesitantly played with too many sub-plots and not enough drive. Sicily was captured, Sardinia left alone, Mussolini fell, Italy surrendered, the allies landed in Italy at Salerno and points south, the Germans took over most of Italy instead of barricading themselves in the north, Mussolini reappeared and – in 1944 by now – the allies hacked their way north, reaching Rome the day before the invasion of Normandy after destroying Monte Cassino on their way. And there was no Act Three. The Italian campaign became a dead end. The most enticing idea for making something more of it was the proposal to push north-east from Italy and sweep into Vienna, but this was not a serious possibility. Churchill, charged then and later with a propensity for spawning bright but impracticable schemes, was not the author of this one, although he was briefly attracted to it provided it could be executed in tandem with *Overlord*. He could not resist a bright idea, but he did not allow himself to be beguiled too far beyond the realities. The main constraint in this case was that the Americans would not have it.

For Churchill Italy was a way of getting at the Germans. The Balkans were another, but both these areas were more than that. Given that Germany must be utterly defeated and that the main thrust of this defeat must be made through northern France, there was nevertheless the barely less cardinal question of the Mediterranean. To his allies and many of his British colleagues the Mediterranean was just a battlefield, but Churchill never forgot that when the battles were over the Mediterranean would still be there. It was as real to him as Europe, perhaps more so. Its closure to British vessels for nearly three years had been one of the war's direst reverses. It was more important than either Italy or Greece for its own sake and this assessment goes far to explain his bizarrely over-optimistic harping on attempts to get Turkey into the war as an active ally. Italian pretensions in Africa might be squashed and the Germans put back on their proper side of the Alps, but behind these practical matters was something else: the assertion of the abiding geopolitical significance of the Mediterranean. And not only the Mediterranean.

The Mediterranean did not stop short at its Syrian shores. It led directly into the Middle East and it might lead into eastern Europe. The Middle East was an active theatre in both World Wars. In the first it figured in a number of ill-related ways from the Turkish declaration of war in November 1914 and the Gallipoli campaign in the next year, to German and Russian operations in the Caucasus and Armenia, to others along the Euphrates, to the Arab Revolt and the capture of Jerusalem. These episodes were, or were believed to be, critical for the outcome of the war (even if their conduct sometimes had a dilettante touch). Churchill had been directly involved in a number of them. Decades later the Middle East and its oil were regarded primarily as profit centres, but for Churchill they were still an integral piece of grand strategy. He had been a member of the Ministry which had taken shares in the first British company to go into Iranian oil – a step at least as significant as Disraeli's purchase of shares in the Suez Canal Company – and had been first lord of the admiralty in the age of the conversion of the Royal Navy from steam to oil. He was an early initiate into the politics of oil. In World War II Middle East oil had not yet attained the paramount position which new discoveries in Kuwait and Saudi Arabia were to give it, but oil was second only to the Atlantic U-boats as the Achilles' heel of Britain's economic survival. Churchill was alive to these short-term and longer-term developments in the shaping of the balance of power in the world. They strengthened his view of the Middle East as an area of central importance – a view formed in the first place by overt events and covert intelligence about German schemes for that part of the world, for Churchill was not the only war strategist with a roving eye.

In Berlin the Abwehr and other bodies had the Middle East in their sights, intriguing with anti-British elements, plotting anti-British sabotage and envisaging – some cautiously, others much less so – anti-British intervention. The central figure, after the chief of the Abwehr Admiral Wilhelm Canaris, was General Helmuth Felmy. Felmy had served in the Middle East in World War I, had been promoted to general on the eve of World War II, had been disgraced in 1940 when he was held responsible for the loss of secret maps and papers relating to the coming invasion of the Low Countries, but had been reinstated a year later (perhaps on account of his special oriental credentials). When in April 1941 an anti-British coup in Baghdad made Rashid Ali al-Gailani the effective ruler of Iraq and a month later the Germans conquered Crete, Felmy was despatched to Baghdad as head of a new military mission which was intended to make Baghdad the headquarters of a new theatre of war of vague but almost limitless extent. Felmy got no further than Aleppo in Syria because, largely owing to Churchill's decisiveness, Rashid Ali's coup was quickly undone. Felmy was repositioned at Sounion, near Athens, whence he directed a more realistic web with tentacles in Syria, Turkey and Iran, before moving in 1942 with a unit several thousand strong to the Caucasus whence he hoped to lead German thrusts towards Basra in Iraq or Teheran or both. In Berlin, where both Rashid Ali and the anti-British mufti of Jerusalem Haj Amin el-Husseini arrived during 1941, these stirring schemes mingled with the even more far-flung ambitions of Subhas Chandra Bose and his Indian National Army. Throughout this period and later the forces opposed to them in the Middle East were overwhelmingly British. In retrospect the threats personified in Felmy may seem unserious, but they could not be so easily brushed off at the time. They were alive in British minds at the date of the Casablanca conference in the winter of 1942–43 and not entirely expunged until the full consequences of the battles of Stalingrad and Kursk in 1943 could be reliably assessed.[4] Churchill did not save Britain's hold on the Middle East but – whether or not that might be a salutary objective or even in the long run possible – he was rightly concerned to prevent its transfer from British to German dominion.

There was, finally, the Middle East as gateway into Europe by what the British thought of as the tradesmen's entrance. This route was turned by Stalin's victories from a possible strategic option into a profoundly political one with implications which were glimpsed by some but fully appreciated at the time by nobody. Churchill fretted and dabbled. His eastern strategies or foibles – call them which you will – were not intrinsically flawed, but they were flawed upon a premise which Churchill unquestioningly accepted: *Overlord*. They were incompatible with *Overlord*, but Churchill never contemplated the abandonment of *Overlord* which was the means by which the Americans, having been brought into the war in Europe, would defeat Germany. *Overlord* was overwhelmingly an American operation which had to be planned and conducted on American lines, one of which was overkill. It has often been alleged that the British in general and Montgomery in particular were over-cautious when it came to risking lives, but in their own way the Americans – then and in wars to come – were at least as much averse to

4. What was not known at the time were the rivalries which played a part in shredding these schemes. The Germans were busy concealing their plans from the Italians to whom Hitler had promised all Arab lands south of Turkey. Rashid Ali and the mufti were on the worst of terms. The Abwehr and the German Foreign Office were also at odds much of the time.

beginning operations until victory had been securely written into the scenario. On this basis the attack on Germany could be launched only across the Channel from England, for there was no other place where the huge forces employed could be assembled. An eastern campaign in tandem with *Overlord* was for the Americans an irrelevance and an irritation. It was a practical possibility only if it both supplanted *Overlord* and could be successfully mounted on a much smaller scale than *Overlord*. It would consequently have been hazardous to the point of folly. Nobody, not even Churchill, ever envisaged anything of the kind and it is impossible even in retrospect to argue that the putative gains could have been held to outweigh the logistical complexities and strategic hazards. Such an operation might have changed the world, but that is not a sufficient reason for arguing that it should have been attempted.

. . .

IV

Churchill's fancifulness could be maddening. Having bright ideas is no bad thing, but having too many and too uncontrolled can be dangerously distracting or positively disastrous. Churchill made life cruelly difficult for his principal commanders and advisers and his sometimes capricious waywardness diminished his credit with his allies. In military matters he behaved like a whole battery of loose cannon. With civil servants he could be most uncivil. His insistence on observing idiosyncratic hours of work was, to say the least, inconsiderate. The Italian campaign, however, was more ill-executed than ill-conceived and its disappointments cannot fairly be laid at Churchill's door. Nor does it cast much light on the ultimately crucial question of Churchill's relations with his principal allies.

Churchill knew and acknowledged to himself that these allies were stronger than he was, but he did not see himself or allow others to see him as a subordinate triumvir. All triumvirs were equal even if some triumvirs were more equal than others. Churchill was assiduous in cultivating Roosevelt's goodwill (not difficult) and in edging him towards war (not easy). He succeeded in getting for Britain a large part of the United States' war production and when Britain ran out of cash to pay for it his good relationship with Roosevelt was fundamental to the approval of Lend Lease by Congress early in 1941 – the next best thing to belligerence. But American belligerence was not his doing. It was brought about by Hitler when, after Pearl Harbor, he committed the egregious error of declaring war on the United States. It is far from certain that the United States – meaning, in this matter, the American president *and* Senate – would have declared war on Germany in support of Britain which, the U-boat campaign apart, was under no great threat; and certain that they would not have done so in support of the Soviet Union. The American way of war was to promise all help short of fighting forces, which was very much the same as Britain's way of making war in the eighteenth century: to pay somebody else to do the fighting, not a bad policy if you can afford it although regarded by some as unmanly.

Having embraced the Soviet Union as an ally half way through 1941 and acquired the United States as another at the end of the year, Churchill's military worries were thereafter compounded by the needs of statecraft on two fronts. His handling of his allies has been criticised and is open to criticism, but neither in relation to the war nor to postwar affairs can it be more than marginally faulted. Like many British leaders Churchill thought that Americans thought of the British as elder brethren with special claims on their siblings in times of trouble, whereas, if a family analogy is to be sought, it was nearer the mark to see the Americans as seeing the British as worthy uncles with some rather deplorable and antiquated bad habits (imperialism and protectionism). There were hints of this discrepancy in the first wartime meeting of Churchill and Roosevelt, but Churchill's extrovert nature belittled all obstacles to comradeship and Roosevelt had no reason to make them explicit; and so long as the issue of the war was in doubt the two leaders ensured that the alliance overrode the inner tensions. Churchill set so much store by the American alliance that he allowed optimism to cloud some realities and created in Britain myths about the Anglo-American relationship which had not existed before the war and were misleading after it. Perhaps he even came to believe that he and Roosevelt so embodied the spirit of the English-speaking peoples that their personal partnership amounted to a political fact. If so, that was an error but not one which impaired the conduct of the war. It may even have helped, although there was a price to pay later for the illusion.

About Stalin Churchill had few illusions, but he had some about his impact on Stalin. Churchill's warm belief in the virtues of personal contacts and shared dangers coloured his diplomacy. Their first meeting was almost a total disaster but also, and significantly, proof that neither could afford a breach at that early stage and they knew it. Criticism of Churchill's dealings with Stalin at a later stage amount to saying that Churchill could and should have been tougher. The main case is Poland. The issues were the constitution of Poland's postwar government – the Poles who had been sitting out the war in London or the Poles in Poland who had been picked by Stalin as adequately subservient to Moscow – and the frontiers of postwar Poland which Stalin wanted to push westward at German expense in order that he might take for himself what had been part of prewar Poland. The principal features of this conflict were Stalin's occupation of Poland as a consequence of the German retreat on the eastern front and Roosevelt's comparative indifference to the Polish question and to European frontiers in general.

The London Poles, to whom Churchill was broadly sympathetic, nevertheless irritated him with their special pleadings, the more so when these complicated his dealings with Stalin. Churchill told de Gaulle on one occasion that in any contest between his French and American allies he would always side with the latter and he did so even when Roosevelt was at his most obtuse over French affairs. And so with the Poles. In eastern Europe Churchill's prime concern was to keep the Russians in the war at least until Hitler's armies had been terminally crippled. Within that concern, but only within it, he would do what he could for the Poles and when the Poles, who naturally were concerned on their side with Poland's future and showed little understanding of Churchill's position, pressed for policies which Churchill would not support he lost patience with them. The problem was not Poland's independence but where it was to be and the fact was that its frontiers were fixed by the timing of the Second Front in the west. If the Americans and British had landed in France in 1943 as many, including the Russians, ardently advocated, the forces determining Poland's future would have been quite different, but since the western allies did not cross the Rhine until 1945 neither the British nor the Americans nor, least of all, the Poles could do much to prevent Stalin from having his own way – that is, installing a Polish government of his choice and fixing Poland's boundaries with the minimum of regard for the arguments of his allies. Churchill was no more than a suppliant begging for concessions and Stalin saw no need to make any. The questions in retrospect are: did Churchill overrate the value of the Russian alliance by 1944 and should he have threatened to break it? For such toughness there were two essential preconditions: Anglo-American agreement and the will to do what was threatened even if it were to cause Stalin to make a separate peace with Hitler.

In spite of the substantial numbers of Poles in the United States Roosevelt was not much interested in Poland. He was on the other hand very much interested in preserving the alliance with Stalin not merely against Hitler but also for a future Russian offensive against the Japanese in China. It is difficult to believe that Roosevelt rated the frontiers of Poland or the virtues of one brand of Polish politician as worth a breach with Stalin and impossible to believe that Stalin would have paid any attention to an ultimatum by Churchill unsupported by Roosevelt. If that is a fair judgement, neither of the two preconditions posed above could be satisfied and the answer therefore to the second of the two questions is no. The first question becomes abstract although it remains intriguing. The fundamental element in Churchill's attitude to Stalin is Churchill's belief that Stalin, whatever else he might be, was a lesser threat than Hitler to Europe and to Britain's position in Europe. Critics of Churchill in this context need to refute that proposition.

Churchill has been accused of more widespread incompetence or betrayal in relation to the rest of eastern Europe. These accusations focus on two meetings: his meeting with Stalin in Moscow in October 1944 and the meeting of the three allied leaders at Yalta in the following February. The charge is that he did not do enough to save eastern Europe (other than Greece) from Stalin's vengeful spoliation and tyranny – that he truckled to Stalin. By October 1944 Soviet armies had entered Romania, Germany, Yugoslavia and Slovakia and had compelled Bulgaria to declare war on Germany.

Roosevelt did not go to the Moscow meeting because of the imminence of the election which was to make him president for the fourth time. There was therefore some uneasiness among Americans about what Churchill might get up to on his own. What he did do was to attempt to limit Stalin's freedom, won by his armies, to dispose of eastern and central Europe as he wanted. Before the Teheran conference in November 1943 Churchill had hoped to impose some such limits by taking a hand, with Americans, in military operations on the eastern front, but by October 1944 any prospect of joint operations of this kind had vanished and the alternative of restraining Stalin by a negotiated deal was feeble and foredoomed to failure.

From around mid-1943 it had been virtually obvious that Stalin's armies were in a position to occupy and control most of Europe east of Germany. Churchill feared that their conquests might even extend to Istanbul and Italy too. What was uncertain was the timing and Churchill pondered the possibility of using the time which might be available to introduce another uncertainty: to make the coming Soviet conquests less than entirely Soviet or, in other words, to get in on the act. Hence his toying with serious operations in the Aegean to be followed by advances into the Balkans, the Danube valley and Austria with (if possible) the help of Turkey and Italy. These schemes may have been altogether chimerical. It is difficult to judge since the Aegean prelude was a flop and the further visions dissolved. In any case the Americans were totally scornful. They were wedded to remaining on good terms with Stalin and feared that the old imperialist Churchill was fighting old Anglo-Russian battles which belonged to a bygone age. Ironically, in view of postwar history, they feared that Churchill was becoming more anti-Russian than anti-German. Churchill therefore was forced to try another tack. Instead of staking a claim by physical presence he fell back on diplomatic wheedling with inevitably reduced horizons. In this endeavour he was probably following Eden whose approach was always more diplomatic than strategic. In the Foreign Office Eden had floated an idea for getting Stalin to renounce any claim to interfere in Greece in return for similar abnegation by Britain in Romania, but he got less than no encouragement from Washington where his notion was treated as a deplorable reversion to the politics of spheres of influence (regarded by Americans as sinful) and meanwhile the Russians occupied Romania (and Bulgaria) and forced King Michael – who had dismissed the pro-German Antonescu regime – not only to accept communists in government (which he had already decided to do), but soon afterwards to abdicate. When Churchill arrived in Moscow in October 1944 Soviet power in these countries was established and Stalin had in effect the freedom to treat all eastern and central Europe, except Greece, as *tabula rasa*. Even earlier, at Teheran, Churchill had concluded that the American refusal to contemplate any serious Anglo-American operations anywhere except in France must produce this result. In Moscow therefore a year later his aim was to devise a clog on Stalin's freedom of action in his conquered and about-to-be-conquered lands.

In the course of their discussions Churchill passed to Stalin a piece of paper on which he had jotted down some figures. This bit of paper has in some accounts been dignified with the name of the 'percentages agreement'. It listed the countries of eastern Europe (other than Poland) and set against each of them two percentages which, Churchill suggested, could be taken to indicate in round figures the relative interests of the western allies and the Soviet Union: thus, Romania 90/10 per cent in the latter's favour, Greece the reverse. Stalin paid, or affected to pay, little heed to this figurative advance and Churchill dismissively retracted it. There was never any agreement nor on Churchill's part an intention to strike a formal or precise bargain. The figures were all but meaningless. Churchill's objective was simply to claim some say for Britain and the United States in whatever might happen in the countries about to become a Soviet sphere. It was a bid not to be left out. At Yalta in February, by which time Budapest too had surrendered to Soviet forces, the western position was even weaker and the best that Churchill and Roosevelt could achieve was agreement on a Declaration on Liberated Europe, a declaration of principles which Stalin ignored as soon as he judged it prudent to do so. To any more binding agreement on eastern Europe he would not have adhered. Churchill and Roosevelt accepted what little they could get at the risk of appearing to be gulled by Stalin. They might have done better to accept nothing, but the climate was still one of slim hopes rather than cynical abandon. Yalta took place a year too far. Half Europe was in Stalin's power. What he would do there depended on how he assessed the current of events which he and his armies had created. He believed that eastern Europe was his *Gau* and so it was, provided only that he kept clear of the Mediterranean.

. . .

V

Great men do not come flawless. Most often none appears at all. In the entire panorama of World War II de Gaulle alone stands beside Churchill as a great national war leader. Churchill was a man of extraordinary stamina and extraordinary courage – two qualities of surpassing value in times of extreme doubt and danger. He possessed a rare capacity for differentiating what was vital from what was merely important, single-mindedness in dismissing compromise when prime issues were at stake, and a striking gift for evoking trust. Winning wars requires something more than arms, brains, discipline, sacrifice and luck; it requires also inspiration and Churchill provided it. He was not a man for all seasons, but he was the man for the brief fraught season which made him immortal.

Chapter 5

FRANCE AND RENEWAL

. . .

I

France entered the war with hesitation, surrendered ten months later after fighting for six weeks and became divided to the verge of civil war. So abject a collapse by so great a Power was almost without parallel in modern European history. The recovery of much of that power was not much less astonishing. It required radical reversals of policies and attitudes grounded in serious and creative reflection.

The French capitulation of June 1940 was psychologically, although not logistically, inescapable. The French government and some of its forces, particularly naval and air forces, could have been removed to North Africa and did start to be so. But logistics are not enough. France did not wish to fight on. It was stunned by the scale and shame of its defeat and it feared anarchy. A quarter of the entire population were refugees; close on 2 million were prisoners or missing; 300,000 had been killed or badly wounded.[1] The government was in disarray and there were rumours of a communist seizure of power in Paris and frightful visions of a second

---

1. The pain did not stop there. Some 60,000 were killed by British air raids on French targets – roughly the same as British casualties from German raids on Britain. The Gestapo inflicted torture and death and from 1943 600,000 Frenchmen were transported to Germany for forced labour. Hence much of the bitter vengefulness against collaborators. Towards the end of the war the Germans resorted to mass reprisals and atrocities against the Resistance and its supposed adherents. The costs of the occupation were set prodigiously high in marks, increased by a 25 per cent devaluation of the franc and exacted from the French.

Commune and a repetition of the lacerations which had followed that other defeat at German hands seventy years earlier: *La Débâcle*. Hitler's attack, launched on 10 May, had precipitated the resignation of the prime minister Paul Reynaud not – as in Neville Chamberlain's case – for the better prosecution of the war but in order to stop it. An armistice was signed on 24 June. France was partitioned. Alsace and Lorraine were detached as a step towards their annexation to Germany; the departments of the north-east were placed under German military government with headquarters in Brussels; northern France and the entire Channel and Atlantic coasts became German-occupied territory under German civil and military authorities in Paris; France south of the Loire was declared a 'free' zone, but pieces in the south-east were allotted to Italy which had joined the war to get them. These dispositions were altered in November 1942 when Anglo-American forces landed in North Africa and the German occupation was extended to the whole of France except the Italian section which, hitherto under Italian supervision only, became Italian-occupied territory.

There was still a French government. When Reynaud was succeeded by Marshal Pétain the government was in flight from Paris via Tours to Bordeaux. After the armistice it chose not to stay in Bordeaux which was in the German-occupied coastal zone and not to return to Paris, although it was entitled to do so and the Germans may have expected and even wished it to do so. It wandered off to central France and settled in Vichy without at first intending to stay there. The existence of this government over the remainder of the war and its location away from Paris were cardinal facts in the history of these years. Vichy represented continuity, for the personalities at Vichy from the Marshal downwards included prominent personages from the civil and military establishments of the Third Republic, and although markedly of the Right, Vichy was not exclusively so. Its legitimacy was more open to question since it depended on votes in a rump parliament which were used undisguisedly to subvert the Republic and create an authoritarian oligarchy. There was, however, no other claimant to legitimacy: the alternative to Vichy was a void. De Gaulle was virtually unknown in France (and elsewhere) and his appeals to French colonial governors and generals fell for the most part on deaf ears. The great majority of the French people was not yet ready to think about the future, for current problems left no space for anything else. The first of these problems was peace and the second was the release and return to France of prisoners of war. Pétain could be relied upon to do his best to turn the armistice into a peace treaty and get the prisoners back. He was plainly a man of order and against chaos and he knew how to look like a head of state: he gave some dignity to an otherwise shabby scene. That for the time being was enough and few wished to ask awkward questions such as whether he was a fascist. Had they put that question as bluntly as historians are apt to do they would probably have concluded that he belonged somewhere in the border-lands between reactionary conservatism and fascism – an apposite illustration of the difficulties of defining a fascist and an omen of what his regime was to become. The simple truth was that Pétain had enormous moral authority. Just how much France had owed to him in 1917 might be a question for experts, but that the debt was large nearly all French men and women correctly judged. Nor was he in 1940 the senile relic portrayed a few years later. He provided spiritual solace in the manner and with the limitations of an icon. There was nobody else who could.

The Vichy regime was undone by contradictions which it could not handle. It became tarnished and demeaned. On the one hand making peace and getting the prisoners back entailed good relations with the Germans, but within two or three years good relations came to mean the conscription of other Frenchmen for forced labour in the German war economy and participation in the wholesale slaughter of Europe's Jews. Furthermore, the extension of the direct German occupation in November 1942 belittled Vichy which was already weakened by the semi-official activities in Paris of pro-German sycophants and fascists who were treated by the Germans in the French capital as alternative channels for doing business in France. So long as the unoccupied zone existed, Vichy had enough authority in enough of France to justify its pretensions and safeguard its popular regard, but the absorption of the unoccupied zone into the occupied zone made it irrelevant. Further, the allied land-ings in North Africa, which precipitated the total occupa-tion, coincided with the death of Pétain's most presentable minister and led to the creation of a rival centre of power on French soil in Africa, a centre which Vichy failed to annex. While events in France in 1942–43 (especially the forced labour) and the dawning possibility of a German defeat turned passive into active Resistance, events in Africa gave de Gaulle the opportunity to turn his office in London into a government-in-waiting in French Algeria.

The second most important man in Vichy was Pierre Laval whom Pétain, in company with many others, did not like. Laval had two strong points: he was clever and he knew how to make himself, if not liked, yet valued. Pétain appointed him prime minister, but dismissed him in December 1940 and he remained out of office but in the wings until April 1942. The reasons for this severance have never been clear. It has been argued that the two men stood for different policies with regard to the big questions of the moment and it is certain that in their characters and backgrounds they differed greatly, but it does not follow that their policies were much different. Both contemplated the future in terms not only of an end to the fighting, but saw the armistice as the prelude to a peace and to alliance with Germany. Pétain, however, quickly came to the conclusion that Laval was taking too much upon himself, getting above his station and treating the marshal as a mere figurehead. But before dismissing Laval, Pétain took the trouble to write to Hitler to get his endorsement, assuring the Führer that French policies would not change and that he would appoint as Laval's successor a politician no less committed to collaboration with Germany. Hitler was angered by Laval's removal, but he was not well informed on French affairs and feared, without good reason, that Pétain was adopting a less compliant stance in Franco-German relations whereas the principal differences between the two Frenchmen lay, first, in Laval's open pro-German and anti-British sentiments and a reserve in Pétain which roused uneasiness in German minds and, secondly, in Laval's willingness to look ahead whereas Pétain was more disposed to take things as they came and let the future look after itself. He did not want to add to his burdens by brooding over the future as well as present misfortunes. Laval on the other hand spent in Pétain's eyes too much time on grandiose schemes for Franco-German cooperation in a postwar Europe which had not yet arrived – a task which seemed ill-judged among the debris and perplexities of wartime France.

Laval's first successor was Pierre-Etienne Flandin, who turned out to be an interlude. Long before the war both Laval and Flandin had seen the sense of ending Franco-German feuding, but in the supremely delicate situation of 1940 Laval was too blatant and Flandin dithered and got nowhere. Both were uncertain about where to conduct Franco-German relations. The joint Armistice Commission had limited competence and humiliating associations. Dealing with the German authorities in Paris meant degrading Vichy and rubbing shoulders with the more outspoken French fascists who were making their pitch around the Nazis' civil and military headquarters in the French capital. What Laval and Flandin most wanted was direct and personal links with Berlin and the Führer's various headquarters, but Hitler was never willing to vouchsafe them this status. He was much less interested in Franco-German reconciliation and partnership than were French politicians.

Pétain's third choice for prime minister was Admiral Darlan who proposed to take a more robust attitude than either Laval, who mixed grovelling with vanity, or Flandin, who seemed content with *attentisme*. Darlan had a different approach to French collaboration. He intended to make the most of France's assets – its navy and empire – and whereas Laval's vision of Franco-German cooperation was a directorate for European affairs, Darlan's was a division leaving the continent to Germany with France and its empire as an intact, separate and equal Power. Whether Darlan might find sympathetic hearers in Germany was uncertain. His vision was like Hitler's with the crucial difference that Hitler aimed to share power with a British, not a French, imperial and overseas Power. In the event Darlan did not last long as prime minister and, largely through German pressures, Laval was reinstalled. But Darlan played one more important part because he found himself accidentally in North Africa in November 1942 when the Americans and British landed and then got killed there on Christmas Eve.

The months of November to February in that winter in North Africa were a turning point in French history. It is not easy to see how that history would have run if the allies had not landed in North Africa. At the beginning of this short period Darlan was the most eminent and most powerful Frenchman on that scene, but also an equivocal one. He was transformed from Vichy's senior representative into the chosen chief – chosen by the allies – of French forces and services and thereby contender for the office of head of state. Algeria was formally part of France, neither a colony nor a protectorate like its Moroccan and Tunisian neighbours. Constitutionally it consisted of departments with the same status as the departments in Corsica and metropolitan France and it contained a substantial French population as well as French forces. With the extension of the German occupation to the whole of France, Algeria became a possible seat for an independent French government, a tactic rejected in 1940. Darlan, being present, was an automatic choice to head such a government and in order to strengthen his claim he put it about that so far from deserting Pétain, he was in Algeria with the marshal's discreet approval. He ordered the French forces in Algeria, which had opposed the allied landings, to rally to the invaders and he assembled a Council of notables which included the governor-general of Algeria and for the first time since 1940 abandoned the policy of Franco-German cooperation. By tilting France away from Germany and towards the Anglo-Saxons, Darlan publicly avowed that Vichy France and Nazi Germany were incompatible. Without abandoning a policy of Franco-German cooperation in the long term, he took sides with those who were thinking of another channel for it, after the defeat of Hitler's Germany and the liquidation of Vichy.

These developments in Algeria stole de Gaulle's clothes. Until the end of 1942 de Gaulle alone had been openly anti-German to the extent of waging war against Hitler, but however valuable he was as a symbol and inspiration, in terms of power he did not count for much. The British paid attention to him largely because he happened to be in London where personally he commanded considerable respect and admiration in spite of being irritatingly insistent on France's deserts and his own claims to embody them. He had character, intelligence, faith but little power to go with them. His first attempt to make a mark in the war resulted in a severe rebuff off Dakar in Senegal and formally he lacked the credentials of the Dutch and Norwegian monarchs ensconced in the British capital or the Belgian ministers who had fled there when their king refused to do so. Within France Resistance (as distinct from the networks which helped escaping prisoners and pilots) was no more than a gleam in optimistic eyes and the Americans, who disliked and distrusted de Gaulle and never ceased to do so, advertised their predilections by maintaining in Vichy an ambassador sympathetic to that regime who had special links to Roosevelt and undue respect for Pétain. The Americans hoped to keep or squeeze de Gaulle out of North Africa by adopting General Henri Giraud as an amenable and respectable puppet *faute de mieux* until Darlan's adventitious arrival a few days before the landings briefly presented them with somebody a good deal *mieux*.

Giraud, who had commanded an army in 1940, was superior to de Gaulle in military rank but inferior in everything else. Darlan made him a member of his Council and on Darlan's assassination at the end of the year Giraud emerged as chief of the burgeoning politico-military French authority teetering on the borders of France like Louis XVIII waiting in Ghent during the Hundred Days to be carried back to Paris in the baggage of the Great Powers. In the new year Roosevelt persuaded the two generals to meet in Casablanca and they became, briefly, co-equal chiefs, but Giraud faded away on account of his political ineptitude, his firm but wrong-headed assessment of the popular mood in France and his mistake in leaving Algiers for a tour of foreign capitals (where he was recognised as no more than just another general). De Gaulle summoned up the patience to let Giraud, who was neither especially intelligent nor especially popular, hang himself.[2] From this point de Gaulle established an unassailable claim to be the government of France. He was assisted by the stirrings of Resistance in France, but his power and his legitimacy came from the shift from Vichy to Algiers of the government-to-be, of which he became the head. Algiers became for him what London could never have been.

2. This was a remarkable exercise in self-control. De Gaulle was outraged by the American collaboration with Darlan, ex-Vichy prime minister; by the appointment of Darlan as high commissioner in North and West Africa; by the promotion of Giraud to those posts and, in addition, to be commander-in-chief of French forces; and finally by the appointment of the peculiarly unacceptable Marcel Peyrouton as governor-general of Algeria.

. . .

II

Modern France has been a conservative country (perhaps all powerful societies are conservative for most of the time) and change has characteristically been delayed by a conservatism which from time to time approaches strangulation. France has then to be jolted rather than eased out of the past into the present. This is a pattern which digs ditches between past and future. As the French Revolution showed, the jolt may be equally effective and disagreeable. World War II was another such jolt. The Franco-Prussian war which came half way between these two supremely critical events was a third, if less penetrating, upheaval. Between these seismic shocks were the intervening periods of slow or very slow change in which the forces of change were repressed until they produced a great commotion. Modern French history presents a pattern of conservatism cherished in their different ways by aristocrats, peasants and bourgeois, but punctured by threats of anarchy. This is a dangerous pattern which requires people who prize continuity and decorum to handle the future by risking and then controlling catastrophes: steady state leading to big bangs. After each big bang there has been a conservative reflux, a recovery of decorum but renewed risks of stagnation.

France was the first of the great European 'nation' states and has been a cynosure throughout the modern era, a state which exalted its own sovereign independence (independence from the papacy, from other states), military prowess and civilised example and dared other states to do better. At its heart was the progressively centralised monarchy which reached its peaks of power and pretension in the seventeenth century and is epitomised by the Versailles of the Roi Soleil. This centralisation of the state was preserved by the Revolution which replaced the absolutist monarchical regime by that of the bourgeoisie, Versailles by Paris, and Latin by French as the country's official language. With the arrival of the industrial and demographic revolutions in the slipstream of the great Revolution, young men trekked to Paris in search of work and careers and young girls into domestic service or brothels – two of the principal appendages of the urbanised bourgeoisie – and, as Balzac demonstrated, an age of bustle-and-gain kept France in the van of modernism in its own eyes and in the eyes of others. But reality began to look different and as the nineteenth century went on bourgeois France found it less easy than the *ancien régime* to hold its own in the world of nation states. Increasingly it competed against the odds.

The centrepiece of the French bourgeois state – whether it had a king or emperor or president – was the French bourgeois family. This unique institution, which has been described as one of the great social inventions in European history, became in the nineteenth century as distinct from the family elsewhere as French poetry became in the seventeenth century distinct from other poetry, and in both cases by a conscious definition and exaltation which gave both the one and the other its special character, strengths and limitations. The French bourgeois family was the central force in French life from the Revolution onwards. As a focus of loyalties it outranked the church, the school, the guild or labour union, the employer corporation, and the state itself in all its manifestations, central or regional. It had abandoned the divisive primogeniture of the *ancien régime* and, uniquely in Europe, accorded equal status to the paternal and maternal lines. It was elastic, reaching through wives and daughters, and it achieved a powerful middle station between the individual and the corporation which suited the ethos of rural life and of early industrialisation. It yoked the nexus of kin with that of cash in a single highly motivated drive. But in economic terms it had a serious weakness. It was a small capitalist unit in control of small agricultural holdings and small businesses, economically successful within its own terms so long as the family could supply not only the labour but also the capital required, but as the economic environment changed it lagged behind the changes and began to act as a brake – the primal capitalist sin. France got stuck in the first stage of the industrial and financial revolutions. In a world where growth was dominant kinship, even on the French bourgeois model, was not enough. In spite of its natural resources and (comparatively) high levels of education, France as a whole – that is to say, France as an economic entity rather than an aggregation of social units – lost ground and began to lose faith in itself. Yet it was reluctant to abandon structures which had become a way of life fortified by the strongest of human bonds, those of the family. There was awareness of the need to catch up with the times and initiate a *relance* but also a melancholic lack of appetite which limited the *relance* to too little and too slow and deprived the future of the excitement which spurred change in other countries. For France the most effective spur came from outside: the German challenge, in arms in 1870 and economically thereafter; the devastation and deaths of World War I; the failures of the Versailles settlement to provide security; the revival of German power and hostility in the 1930s. A second war bade fair to be a make-or-break affair. By this date recovery required more than victory. It required also thorough economic reform and a radical re-view of French relations with Germany and the French position in Europe.

Besides ending the war and partitioning the country, the armistice of 1940 imposed on France a period of reflection. The conflict between pro- and anti-Vichyssois provided a framework, but within the frame most French men and women neither took sides nor felt compelled to do so. In a country at war most people think and talk about the day's rumours and events: the present is an all-absorbing topic. But France was no longer at war except in a technical sense and Resistance operations, when they took shape, were con-fined to the few. France suffered no mass slaughter of its brightest and best as it had in the earlier conflict, and after the initial shock of humiliation and confusion there was room for some minds to turn to what was going to happen when it was all over. Both Vichy and the Resistance were as angry with France's prewar leaders as they were with their German occupiers, critical of their own past and not keen to get back to it. French people probably thought more about the postwar future than other belligerents – and it helped that, unlike others, in Greece for example, they were not starving. At Vichy and in the Resistance people came to different – bitterly different – conclusions, but they started from the same premises and, being united in their condem-nation of the Third Republic, had more in common than they would have cared to admit.

The task of any French government in the early 1940s went beyond that of getting out of an unwanted and calamit-ous war with the least damage. If, as men and women of all political persuasions believed, there was something radically wrong with France, the war presented an opportunity as well as a warning – perhaps a last opportunity – to put things right. There were two overriding and interconnected worries: that France was no longer up to date and needed a Renaissance, and the fear that France was losing its standing in Europe and needed not only to keep its place on the map, but to earn its place at Europe's top table where it had axiomatically occupied a *fauteuil* for centuries.

The first of these worries was often summarised with the word modernisation. But a Renaissance is by definition backward-looking. The High Renaissance which traditionally separates the modern world from the Middle Ages in (western) Europe looked back to the values and ways of thought of the ancient world as surely as it extended the knowledge and techniques available to future generations, and in this respect Vichy's reactionary nostalgia and prejudices contributed to the renewal of France in the mid-twentieth century. Much of Vichy's thought was muddled, narrow or vengeful, and some of it repulsive, but Vichy also raised questions which needed to be raised and were subliminally present in many minds. The Vichy *mélange* came uncomfortably close to fascism even though few individual fascists found favour in the marshal's entourage. Vichy's programme for cleansing France included purging it of Jews, Freemasons, communists and metics. Vichy mirrored a widespread disgust with the politics and politicians of the Third Republic, but it did not disavow the republicanism which was among the principal legacies of 1789 and denotes in French what other countries call democracy. Vichy condemned modern industrial capitalism, its indifference to any but material criteria, its irresponsibility, its megalomania. It did so in response to the gut feeling – Vichy's thinking tended to come from the gut rather than the mind – that large is ugly and doom-laden. It could find no better remedy for France's slide down the material and moral ladders than to praise and favour the family farms and businesses, many of which had begun before the war to see the need to transcend family limits: for example, in the wine business which straddled the rural and industrial worlds and personified French enterprise even more than Chanel or Peugeot. Vichy was the backward part of the French Renaissance and at the same time negative; it drew no useful conclusions from its retrospection. The fault of Vichy lay not in looking back but in failing to create anything worthwhile by doing so.

The French did not love their political parties and with the *débâcle* these parties conveniently took the full force of blame as Napoleon III did after Sedan. But Vichy's attempt to forge a new political order was a conspicuous failure partly because Vichy was never wholehearted about anything new but more on account of its inglorious posture in the new German order: an apt fate consigned Vichy's last ministers to a last seat at Sigmaringen where the first Hohenzollerns came from. The Resistance, putting camaraderie before party, believed that the old parties could be abolished and replaced by the unity which the various groups and factions within the Resistance tried to achieve among themselves. It was a foolish vision and Simone de Beauvoir's novel *Les Mandarins* reflects its political naivety. The old parties came back after the war inevitably since they represented different beliefs and attitudes and democracy requires an organised debate around them, not a pretence that they do not exist. The *résistants* failed to distinguish between party political factiousness on the one hand and the inherent weakness of French democracy as it had developed since the Revolution on the other: they aimed to get rid of dirty water by taking the taps off the bath. The men of 1789 and their successors of the triumphant bourgeoisie after 1815 feared strong central government. They believed in government by a popular assembly with the executive as the assembly's executive arm: more democracy than government. France therefore failed to achieve the political stability or the central direction which Britain achieved in the first decades of the eighteenth century. Between the wars of the twentieth century right-wing government was regarded as too strong to be safe, left-wing government as too red to be safe.[3] This pattern seemed set to recur after the war but the

---

3. This was part of the communist legacy after 1919 when the Left split into communists and socialists. The communists had no interest in reforming democratic politics. By camping out on the democratic stage and occupying it, they prevented the socialists from winning power. In default of winning power the socialists strove for a share of it, as too did other parties. Politicking overlaid governing.

inability of governments or assemblies to cope with, above all, decolonisation brought back de Gaulle and a new constitution. De Gaulle, who was no Vichyssois nor a fully committed *résistant* either, wanted strong government, but he was no statist. He wanted a compromise between the *étatisme* of Louis XIV and the populism of the Revolutionary tradition and he went some way to inaugurating it. He recognised and applauded the strength of the *patrie* – which, contrary to assorted Anglo-Saxon beliefs, is not the French word for the state, but more a home, an aspect of the bourgeois emphasis on the primacy of social and cultural emotions and institutions. Unlike *étatisme* it loosens political discourse by taking the rigid definitions of the state (legal and territorial) out of the idea of the nation and by concentrating loyalties on an idea rather than a hard and fast area on a map or jealously protected symbols such as a flag or exchange rates.

More important for Renaissance was economic renovation. French production reached a prewar peak in 1929 and then halved. Production fell to a third of the American level. The modernisation of industry and agriculture, technically and financially; the extension and expansion of education, particularly technical education; and the allocation of such resources as France might find to hand after the war – all these demanded bold and intelligent thinking and got it from a leader hardly less out of the ordinary than de Gaulle: Jean Monnet, the godfather of modern France. Monnet came from a bourgeois family with a well-established family business (cognac) which was conservative but prosperous. He took the high road of French education – *lycée, grande école* – as a prelude to a career in the wide world of private finance. Then the family business got into trouble, not through any scandal or any decline in the quality of its product, but because of weaknesses in its marketing, management and financing. Monnet was called in to put things right, did so, handed over the reins to other members of the family and returned to Paris. In 1939 he had passed fifty. He spent the first part of the war mainly in London or Washington, the latter part between Algiers and Washington. He and de Gaulle recognised one another's qualities and talents, but more warily than warmly. On Monnet's side there were, it seems, some persistent reservations about the trustworthiness of a general in the affairs of a democratic republic. During the war Monnet developed in parallel ideas for the regeneration of France and, as a necessary corollary, ideas about Franco-German relations and Europe. His plans for French economic reform went hand in hand with what were to become the Schuman Plan for the Franco-German steel industries and, beyond that, European Union.

With a small group of carefully picked disciples of outstanding intelligence and practical ability, Monnet prepared the Plan which, named after him, laid the foundations for an economic revolution which produced a French miracle to match the more celebrated German *Wirtschaftswunder*. The Monnet Plan was a strategy. At its heart was government direction but not big government. Although a conservative businessman, Monnet did not trust private capitalism alone to produce national prosperity. He diagnosed as crucial the failure of the capitalist system in the 1930s to provide the requisite investment needed by the economy and he saw that risk capitalists no longer took risks. But the consequent need for state intervention left open the question: how much intervention and how. Monnet did not propose simply to substitute the state and state capitalism for private businesses with their own institutions and initiatives. In his scheme the state was to take as much action (and Monnet was a man of action as much as a thinking man) as was needed to activate economic enterprise whether public or private. He saw no virtue in allowing the state to hog the action in the manner of communism or of fascist corporatism. His central machine was housed in a small government office and its task was to set priorities in the economy sector by sector, by successive five-year plans, and to ration material and financial resources. He himself was at the head of the *Commissariat du Plan* without being a minister or subordinate to any minister except the prime minister. Execution was left to other bodies, public or official, Parisian or provincial: an incidental effect was to halt the economic predominance of Paris and the surrounding region. Besides demonstrating that capitalist planning was not a contradiction in terms, Monnet created a regime in which powerful corporations could flourish and smaller businesses continue to exist.

The Monnet Plan had nevertheless a dreadful gap. It required money for investment in industry beyond the current means of the French economy. The gap was bridged by Marshall aid, much of which was directed on Monnet's advice into the budget of the *Commissariat*. The resurrection of West Germany was likewise primed and underpinned by American money and the similarities did not end there. In both countries native statesmanship and American money combined to fashion a distinctive capitalism with a strengthened emphasis on cooperation between government, capital and labour in place of the older and more combative model which persisted in the United States and Britain and assumed an endemic conflict between capital and labour. In the comprehensive muddle which was Thatcherism, one of the prime tenets of economic policy was an indiscriminate assault on labour unions ranging from statutory regulation of their sometimes undemocratic practices, through measures to control or retard their traditional demands for better wages and working conditions, to a broad attack on their ancillary political activities, financial viability and their very existence. Against this view of economics as a battleground, the French model – and the more radical German model which legislated for labour representation on the boards of companies – aimed to reduce wasteful strife within the system, to institute some interplay between the needs of the economy and those of society, and to strengthen unions against disruptive minorities of the far Left.

In Monnet France found a statesman of great intelligence with an unusual talent for being sensible and an equally unusual talent for linking his country's national problems with their international context. No less a patriot than businessman and financier, Monnet saw French security and French prosperity as parts of one problem. On this view Alsace and Lorraine, which Hitler had once more detached from France in 1940 for reincorporation into Germany, posed a problem of integration, not of frontier-shifting. The Coal and Steel Community, created in 1952 and credited to Robert Schuman, was hatched by Monnet during the war as both desirable in itself and a stepping stone to a European Union. If, as he believed, a United States of Europe was not yet attainable, France and Britain should work together to go as far as practicable in that direction with a free trade zone and some abandonment of sovereignty as a necessary immediate minimum. Monnet's wartime thoughts were directed in equal measure to the regeneration of France and the ridding of

Europe from the demons of nationalism. He might not have been surprised by the laggard pace of achievement, but he would have been saddened and perhaps irritated by the shuffling pettiness and mediocrity which dictated that pace.

. . .

III

In its external affairs France depended in the first place on who won the war and so, increasingly as the war went on, on the United States and Britain. Ultimately, however, the fortunes and fate of France depended on its relations with Germany and on a transformation of French attitudes to Germany. From Richelieu to Napoleon and beyond, France sought to keep the Germans from uniting in a single 'nation' state which would be more than a match for the French state, but with the rise of Prussia and the creation by Prussia of a German empire this strategy failed. Between the Franco-Prussian war and World War II nobody in France could think of an alternative strategy so that the main aim – to weaken Germany by fragmenting it – remained unchanged and progressively more futile.

Franco-German relations were regarded by many French and Germans and by practically everyone else as set in hostility. This was an exaggeration. From Madame de Staël to Romain Rolland French voices had proclaimed the excellence of German culture, and in the political field an Austrian alliance had been a mainstay of French policy during much of the eighteenth century and of Talleyrand's policies both as Napoleon's foreign minister and at the Congress of Vienna after Napoleon's fall. But from the nineteenth century France was affected in a special way by the German problem. The German problem was not peculiar to France, but it affected France peculiarly. The problem arose from the combination of Germany's central location in Europe and its military might. When Prussia took Austria's place as the leading German Power and Bismarck created the Second German Reich, which was Prussia writ large, he linked strategic advantage with great power and so automatically challenged France which had been Europe's premier state from the seventeenth century onwards. The Franco-Prussian war dramatised this challenge. For France the crucial difference between Austria and the Habsburg empire on the one hand and Prussia and the new Reich on the other was that the former could be made to look east against the Turks while the latter could not so easily be diverted from the west: in other words Austria was no menace, but Prussia/Germany was, and the logic of this new order in Europe propelled France towards alliance with Russia. Yet after 1870 France ceased surprisingly quickly to be obsessed with the loss of Alsace and Lorraine, at least to the extent of ceasing to be minded to make war for their recovery: Paul Déroulède, the most vibrant champion of *revanche*, ceased to be a figure of consequence by 1900 at the latest. Long before 1914 Germany's main adversary was not France but Britain. World War I is often treated as the first half of a European conflict of which World War II supplied the second half, but titles of wars are misleading and World War I could just as well be regarded as the second act in a two-act drama which began with the Franco-Prussian war. By 1939 France and Germany had no territorial claims against one another, Hitler did not declare war on France and France went to war with Hitler without any conviction that it was in the French national interest to do so.

The stretch of years between the two great wars of the twentieth century was shaped by the Versailles settlement and its failure to address Europe's German problem. Versailles and associated treaties fiddled with frontiers and punished Germany, but it kept the main question off the agenda: how to fit Germany into the European political system. For centuries the principal mechanism for regulating European affairs had been a self-conscious mobile in which the various Powers and their minor adjuncts manoeuvred so that, by their permutations, the positive ambitions of a major Power or alliance would be inhibited by a flock of support to a negative pole. This was the European states system and Europe's statesmen were its managers; but it could not be managed if circumstances decreed a permanent inferiority of the negative pole. Which by the time of World War I they did. Even Bismarck, who hoped that they would not – at any rate so long as he himself was around – could not alter the circumstances and in 1914 Germany went to war undeterred by the alliance against it of France, Russia and Britain. The fact that Germany lost overall was less ominous than the fact

111

that it won in the east and nearly won in the west. At Versailles the omens were ignored. From the French point of view Versailles was a dead end. It fostered pessimism in France at least as much as indignation in Germany.

France came badly out of both wars. In the first most of the fighting in the west took place on French soil, the French armies suffered unimagined casualties and mutinied, and the peace left France denuded and pessimistic. There were two ways of handling the German problem: to tame Germany's spirit or to clip its claws and hope that they would not grow again. Both assumed that the European states system must persist; nobody not easily certifiable as a crank went so far as to recognise that the problem was rooted in the system. The first solution, however, was a form of unsupported optimism which left everything to chance or providence. The mind of Germany might be changed, even changed permanently: let us hope so but who can tell the future? The second solution was adopted and Versailles deprived Germany of its armed forces and some territory, but could not deprive it of its inherent strengths and its capacity to reverse indignities and discard shackles and reappear as the ringmaster of a states system. The Versailles settlement was no more than a bid for time without any idea of what to do when time was up. The new League of Nations and the untested doctrine of collective security might be a help, but with the United States backing out and Germany excluded for the time being the collective did not amount to much more than France plus Britain, an entente no more serviceable from the French point of view than the lapsed Franco-Russian alliance.

The French recognised the precariousness of the situation and tried to improve it by finding in the east a clutch of allies who would take the place of Russia in the dismantled balance of power. These allies – Poland and the Little Entente in east-central Europe – were beneficiaries at the losers' expense of the territorial reorganisation of Mitteleuropa, enemies of Germany in particular and vulnerable to German pressures if Germany were to become better able than France to bully them economically: which it did. In the League of Nations France had little confidence even before the crises in Manchuria and Ethiopia exposed the shortcomings of collective security and the inevitability of discordant national interests. The defection of Italy to Germany, the Spanish Civil War and the threadbareness of the Little Entente completed the dispiriting of France. The symbol of these years was the Maginot Line, a fence to keep the Germans out which was, however, open-ended and obstructed no Germans in 1940.

The war which ensued was for most French people exceptionally short and pointless. Hitler was no doubt repulsive, but what he wanted was far away. As he had made clear in *Mein Kampf*, published in 1925–26, he wanted territory for Germany in the east and the permanent weakening of other states. His racial prejudices about the malignity of Jews and the inferiority of Slavs and other non-Aryans might fuel his resolve, but the core of his external policies was his compulsive belief in Germany's need to expand to the east, to became bigger so that Germans, who were to increase to 200 million, might have more elbow room, more natural wealth and a superior way of life. He aimed to re-order the European states system in a way which would leave France intact, but (like all other states) diminished. In 1940, when a German victory throughout Europe seemed assured, that was as much as the French people could hope for. Politicians such as Laval might aspire to a more influential partnership with Germany, but were in no position to press for it since they had nothing much to offer.

There was nothing intrinsically discreditable about a Franco-German entente but, like the Versailles settlement, Vichy's approach merely tinkered with the German problem from a position of impotence and as the fortune of war turned against Germany, as Vichy faded and de Gaulle triumphed, the German problem was temporarily subordinated to another. From 1943 onwards de Gaulle won a dominant position among the French at home and abroad, but France's claim to a place at Europe's top table depended on his standing in Washington and London and he never won the willing recognition of the United States. Poorly informed and poorly advised, Roosevelt gave rash support to Vichy for as long as he could and then allowed a barren interlude to persist in American policies on French affairs until a few months before the war ended. Roosevelt's hostility began in ignorance and was confirmed by distrust. He suspected de Gaulle of being some sort of right-wing military dictator of the kind with which Americans were familiar in Latin America. The Wilsonian crusading streak in this complex and sometimes careless politician told him that de Gaulle – whose aloof independent bearing was no recommendation in a political milieu where folksiness was a major virtue – was not the man to back. He envisaged for France after *Overlord* an Anglo-American government on the model first introduced in Sicily and he refused until October 1944 to recognise the French National Committee in Algiers over which de Gaulle presided as the provisional government of France. But de Gaulle had by this time created a broad national unity, armed forces and plans for the assumption of government in the wake of *Overlord* and *Anvil* (the secondary invasion of France in the south in August). Political life sprang into being at all levels – central, departmental and local; careful preparations in London and Algiers together with euphoria helped to ensure good enough relations between those returning from overseas and those who had endured the war at home; even the bitterness against collaborators and the purges were kept or brought under a degree of control.[4] France emerged from the war as a state in command of its own institutions and determined to have a say of some weight in matters beyond its borders. It did so with massive distrust of the United States and also of Britain which, quite apart from having sunk much of the French navy at Mers el-Kebir (the modern equivalent of the Fashoda crisis on the Nile in 1898), was cast as an American satellite.

World War II produced no counterpart to the Treaty of Versailles. This outcome seemed at the time messily

4. The purges were haphazard and far from fair. They were private retribution and arbitrary justice. Probably 4–5,000 people were killed. But for the most part proceedings were handled by authority. Special purge commissions dismissed or penalised over 10,000 public servants. A special *Haute Cour de Justice* for the trial of heads of state and government, ministers at and below cabinet level and colonial governors received between March 1945 and July 1994 108 indictments, tried 49 of them, imposed 17 death sentences of which three (Laval, Darnand, de Brinon) were carried out and pronounced three acquittals; most of the accused were sentenced to civil degradation or prison, two of them for life, two for 20 years, others for 2–10 years (some sentences were suspended). In lower courts over 100,000 persons were brought to trial as part of the resolve to purify France.

inconclusive: wars are supposed to end with treaties which mark the verdict of war and tidy up some of the disarray. But conferences between the principal victors failed to agree on the terms of a peace treaty with Germany and were abandoned after 1947. The breakdown of the anti-German alliance and the onset of the Cold War drove France into impotent acquiescence in a bisected Europe which it abhorred. Russia, eliminated in World War I, became the enemy at the end of World War II. Schemes for neutering Germany (such as the Morgenthau Plan for turning it into a nation of pastoralists, briefly endorsed by Roosevelt and even more briefly by Churchill) were discarded, but the restoration of (western) Germany, its economic reinvigoration and even its rearmament were promoted by the United States with disconcerting speed. All these processes seemed, as the prefix 're' affirmed, to be putting Germany back where it had been when it started the war.

Germany's French and other neighbours were alarmed. The 1930s were not where they wanted to be. Something more radical was needed. French foreign policy drew on two traditions which were more universalist than nationalist and had survived beneath the surface during the heyday of the nation state. The French Revolution proclaimed the Rights of Man, not the Rights of Frenchmen, and it had been for export. Although the export successes – to the Low Countries and Switzerland – were minor and did not last long and were perverted by Napoleon (who exported power rather than ideas), there remained a supranational sediment. A second sedimentary universalist tradition survived from the medieval Christian notion of an imperial superstate in which the territorial prince would be subordinated to the spiritual authority of a Christian pope or, in some versions, emperor such as Charlemagne with his ambiguous nationality – or both in tandem. This notion of a unified Christendom, similar to the Muslim notion of the Dar ul-Islam as a political as well as a religious entity, never came within a million miles of fruition: it excluded Eastern Christianity, popes and emperors were too often at loggerheads, communications were too poor to sustain so wide an empire, common interests too feeble, vernacular languages already divisive and so on. But the dream retained a romantic and utopian niche, particularly in bad times and particularly in the middle ground or great rift formed by the Rhine and in the sentimental make-up of Roman Catholic leaders in that part of Europe which covered the Cologne of Adenauer, the Alsace of Robert Schuman, not to mention the Cross of Lorraine. This dream stirred again when French *étatisme* crumbled in the eighteenth century and the bourgeois state stumbled in the twentieth. To Americans and British it meant nothing.

Midway in the twentieth century these atavistic and per-enially impracticable musings acquired a firmer substance and a daring purpose. It might be that the way to prevent the recurrent onslaughts of the German state on its neigh-bours was to redesign Europe by subordinating the states system to some superior union or federation. The idea was not entirely new, but it had been a marginal fantasy ped-dled by cranks innocent of political sense and it had found no favour with politicians or peoples. (It had made some progress among industrialists and financiers, not however because they liked the idea but rather because they had no time for ideas and were following their business noses.) The European federal idea was first seriously promoted by politicians during World War II when Dutch and Belgians, however much they feared German power, knew that it could not be permanently curtailed and knew too that their coun-tries needed a strong rich Germany to buy their products. The critical issue was whether France would adopt the same view, for without France a European union would be but a big step towards a Greater Germany, an enhancement of the states system but more unbalanced – in Germany's favour – than ever before. The issue was problematical. The Cold War thrust purely military alliance to the forefront of international affairs and worked against union in western Europe if only because union of a peculiarly calamitous kind was what the Soviet Union imposed on eastern Europe. Yet France chose alliance with Germany and, in the Schuman Plan for a European Coal and Steel Community, alliance with explicit federalist implications. This was the forerunner of the Treaty of Rome of 1957 which created the European Economic Community (EEC) which was to become by the Treaty of Maastricht the European Union (EU). This startling reversal of the patterns of a thousand years was due to France more than any other state, for without French concurrence –

as all German chancellors from Adenauer to Kohl feared – there could be no European Union as envisaged by the Treaty of Rome but, the only alternative, a new German Reich.

The impediments were large. De Gaulle's attitudes were ambiguous, if only because he was never a man to parade his views. It was part of his strength as a statesman that he kept people guessing, not so much from calculated deviousness as from an innate aversion to blather. Although unyielding, he was no bigot and too intelligent to allow dogma or stubbornness to be the ultimate governors of his actions. Thus he disliked NATO but accepted it while trying (unsuccessfully) to alter the way it was run. He also disliked the way the EEC had been structured but he was not opposed to union as such and his main goal of a permanent accord with Germany and its nearest neighbours at least implied an economic and political union of some sort. His celebrated advocacy of '*l'Europe des patries*' is a red herring because, if ever he used the phrase (which is doubtful), *patrie* is not the French for state and is commonly used not in reference to the French people as a whole but, in the plural, to the several *patries* within the French state.

Deeper than these niceties were France's historical legacies, for France had to come to terms not only with the defeat of 1940 but also with the long years of defeatism which preceded the war and the loss of empire and imperial illusions which followed it.[5] Yet France found the resolution to espouse permanent collaboration with Germany and the emasculation of the European states system based on state sovereignty. The Treaties of Rome and Maastricht were the bold counterparts to the Second Treaty of Versailles that never was: the winding up of World War II.

. . .

IV

France was an essential element in any plan to integrate western European states after World War II because, although neither victorious in any real sense nor powerful, history had made it important and in 1945 it was more prominent

---

5. Britain shed its colonies but not its illusions or their cost.

than it had seemed in 1940 ever likely to be. But when it was admitted to the magic circle of the United States, the Soviet Union and Britain, it was occupying a position which must sooner or later belong to Germany. Willingly or subliminally France was keeping a seat warm for Germany and hoping to slide into an approximately equal seat when the dust of war settled. Thanks to Jean Monnet its pretensions were not unsound. From the end of the war to the 1970s manufacturing industry, agriculture, retail trade and the balance of payments all flourished, but the oil crises of the 1970s exposed France's vulnerability and initiated a series of inconsistent economic policies focused on rising inflation and unemployment and the inevitable concomitant of public discontent. Franco-American relations remained bad, the French joyfully quick to voice resentment against American commercial predators, cultural invasion and wayward foreign policies. Affronted by Thatcher's ill-mannered xenophobia and alarmed by post-Soviet disintegration in eastern Europe and Russia itself, France became, in fact if also by choice, irreversibly committed to Germany and German policies, including the rapid development of European union at whatever cost. France had moved from a pioneering to an ancillary role in Europe: its voice was heeded but its options were few. The 1980s and 1990s saw an end to cheap food, cheap energy and cheap credit. The collapse of the Soviet empire in Europe precipitated German unification (against which Mitterrand reacted briefly with dismay) and spawned up to a dozen possible applications for membership of the EU by central and eastern European states, all of them seeking from the EU more than they would put into it. Doubts arose about France's ability to sustain the role of Germany's principal junior partner on the road to a European union on Treaty-of-Rome lines. Yet the Franco-German alliance was not so one-sided as material calculations might suggest, for Germany had no ally of the same stature as France nor any which it trusted so firmly. Meanwhile, amid these doubts, two unsettling ghosts appeared as if to warn that past demons do not easily lose their power to frustrate hopeful change. They were fascism and the German Question.

Chapter 6

WHAT HAPPENED TO FASCISM?

. . .

I

World War II has frequently been labelled a war against fascism which ended with the defeat of fascism. Neither statement is true, nor is either completely untrue.

The war in Europe was a war against Germany and various allies, among which Italy was the most important. Italy entered the war in the mistaken belief that it was as good as over and won by Germany: the initiative came from Italy. Britain and France declared war on Germany (which later declared war on the United States) because they feared the power of the German state. Their aim was to curb that power. They did not declare war because Germany had become a fascist state.

Nevertheless Germany and Italy were fascist states and this fact affected those who were called on to fight them. Churchill and other British leaders habitually referred to the chief enemy as Nazis. (The French, however, more often called them Germans and have continued to do so when talking about the war.) Many anti-fascist combatants cared more and understood more about the odious behaviour of their fascist enemies than about the balance of power in Europe. Since, moreover, Germany and Italy were defeated there is some sense in pronouncing that the fascism which they represented so prominently suffered defeat, at least temporarily.

The immediate prelude to the outbreak of war in 1939 was the German-Soviet pact of August 1939 which created an alliance between Europe's leading fascist and communist states. This alliance did not last and, on the German side, was not meant to. In 1941 the Soviet Union, invaded by Germany, became allied with the British and – a few months later – with the American democracy, also temporarily and for the specific and limited purpose of defeating Germany: much of what happens in war is temporary. For half a century after the war international affairs were conducted largely in terms of democracy versus communism. So what happened to fascism?

What is fascism? It is a generic term which is hard to define, but to leave it undefined is to allow it to become an indiscriminate term of abuse. It is characteristically militant but not all militancy is fascist and calling louts or communists fascist devalues the word and confuses the issues. Fascism embraces both a set of ideas and a form of political action. It can be gauged by either of these criteria, but neither is sufficient to explain it without the other. Some of the ideas are essential to fascism and common to all fascist movements, but a particular movement may be marked by ideas which are to be found in other parts of the fascist family only subliminally or not at all.

As a set of ideas fascism is essentially reactionary and revolutionary, not merely conservative. In conventional political terms it is of the Right but it is also hostile to the basic principle of conservatism which seeks to preserve rather than destroy. Fascism is iconoclastic, conservatism is not. Fascism deprecates and aims to undermine established institutions of the state, the economy and society; conservatism does the opposite. Fascists vie with conservatives for the chief place on the Right, each trying to use and ultimately subjugate the other – a hazardous process in which each risks being engulfed by the other. Their conflict is the more confusing and bitter because fascism and conservatism overlap in practice and in spite of their essential enmity: some conservatives are fascists and some fascists are conservatives and many in both camps spare no time bothering about the difference. Fascism is dictatorial and antagonistic to pluralism. A fascist movement seeks to appropriate the state and it distrusts churches, the professions, the intelligentsia and the bureaucracy.

Fascism is anti-rational in the sense that it places the will and the instinct above reason and morality as guides to conduct, and it is anti-democratic because it despises individual rights as clogs on the dynamic of the fascist corporate genius.

Discontent, amounting at times to rage, with the modern world is a prominent feature of fascism and the main source of fascist violence. From the seventeenth century onwards western Europe has pioneered great and accelerating increases in knowledge and techniques which, coinciding with the equally unprecedented growth of the population, have been used to exploit latent resources which had been surplus to the requirements of the medieval world. This upheaval – the age of reason uneasily yoked with the age of the masses – created a mental and social revolution which devalued medieval ruling classes and tended to destroy familiar spiritual landmarks. Fascists react against this modern world, proclaim a mission to purify the modern state and society, and appeal to the large and varied audience comprising all those who have been diminished, damaged or dismayed by it. The fascist mission automatically confers a mystic right which is intolerant, unquestionable and self-justificatory. Given the right adventitious circumstances it becomes also self-fulfilling. Fascism is consequently more than an ideology. It requires a leader with a following which, in the age of the masses, is necessarily a mass following.

A mass movement consists of a mass and a mover: both are essential. A mass movement has therefore some of the elements of a religion, for *religio* is literally what a mover does to a mass – bind and hold it together. What fascists most prize is their movement and its leader, whom they love, venerate and obey. Most fascists have relatively little use for ideas. Since movements move, fascism is committed to action and despises reflection as a waste of time and spirit, a betrayal of the movement's pragmatic purpose which it pursues with a unique blend of ancient mysticism and modern techniques – the mass rally, mass propaganda, mass forces on the march to somewhere. The purpose of the march is to gather more mass and turn it into power and therewith eliminate or subjugate all institutions, parties, unions or other dissentients who may obstruct fascist dominance. Fascism is totalitarian and does not baulk at violence: most fascist leaders have openly extolled violence. This lust for the monopoly of power begins at home but may with opportunity transcend the borders of the state.

Fascism is not necessarily racist or anti-Semitic, but it is predisposed to be so by its narrow and self-regarding exclusivity.

121

It is also so predisposed by the addiction to violence which makes fascists care little about the appalling suffering which racism and anti-Semitism entail. Conservatives are apt to contemplate with some equanimity the misfortunes of others, but fascists are more than untroubled; they accept in advance the need for these ills and even relish them. European fascists espoused anti-Semitism where it was useful to them (in England, for example) or where Jews were especially numerous and moving into positions of prominence in the middle classes (as in parts of central and eastern Europe). For Hitler anti-Semitism was an obsession which gave German fascism its distinctive badge of infamy – Nazism without anti-Semitism is inconceivable – but by contrast Corneliu Codreanu's fascist Iron Guard in Romania was peculiarly unsuccessful in areas with a high proportion of Jews, and Romanian anti-Semitism, which was virulent, was the hallmark of a different and rival party. In Italy, one of the few countries where fascism was successful, anti-Semitism was a belated accretion when Italy became politically, militarily and ideologically annexed to Nazi Germany. Another characteristic but not essential hallmark of fascism is imperialist aggression. Hitler's expansionism was driven by his second obsession: Germany's need for *Lebensraum*. Although imperialism may flourish mightily without fascist trappings, it sits easily with fascism's self-regarding vanities and raucous nationalism. Mussolini's imperialism was fuelled by his jealousy of the French and British empires and his contempt for the Ethiopians whom he gassed with as little compunction as Hitler showed when he resolved to bring the number of Slavs in the world down by 20 million.

Nationalism is eagerly prayed in aid by fascists, the more effectively since nationalism has many virtues. It brings and holds people together, it provides a powerful sense of identity, it helps individuals and societies to fulfil themselves and sets practical and noble aims. It has shaped Europe's borders and, no less, its cultures. But nationalism is a portmanteau word with protean appeal, much of it disreputable. The nation is an aggregate of individuals and so kin to such terms as The People, *Le Peuple, Das Volk*. Kinship is its basic cement and language the most obvious outward sign of this kinship. A national identity is characteristically expressed in and treasured for its buildings, manners, poetry, myths. It is commonly both proud and jealous. Its attributes range from just pride to arrogant or witless contempt. With the coming of the 'nation' state nationalism became also a political term defined by geography and institutions and inheriting from the pre-national, dynastic state a lust for power and a proclivity to belligerence which have been the bane of modern Europe, particularly where it is laced with religion (in southeast Europe, for example). For all its virtues it has no moral rudder and frequently tries to reconcile its rigid ideologies with slippery opportunism. Fostering ill will, distrust and even hatred between people and states, and seducing political leaders into vicious demagoguery, it is a great killer which numbers its dead in hundreds of thousands and creates refugees by the million.[1]

It is useful to recall fascism's definition of itself. The *fasces*, the symbol of consular authority in ancient Rome,[2] were a bundle of rods clustered around a central instrument, which was an instrument of chastisement. They were a symbol of power claiming respect, demanding obedience and instilling fear. At the core of fascism is fear – the fear inseparable from the threat of suppression which, obversely, is a threat to freedom. One of the hallmarks of fascism is the lavish use of gaols as instruments of political and social cleansing.

The main source of fascism's prevalence in Europe between the two World Wars was the fortuitous combination of fascist ideology with anti-communism and the Depression. Without the special circumstances created by communism and economic collapse fascist ideas and parties would in all probability have remained curiosities of merely modest practical significance. Although the Bolshevik Revolution of 1917 turned out not to be catching, it long remained hypnotic: anti-communism was one of the determining factors in European politics throughout Europe for the rest of the century. Communist revolutions in Germany (and Hungary) were quickly defeated and the Left in Europe was lastingly weakened by the split between communists and socialists in

1. Militant nationalists are not above courting nationalists of a different stripe from themselves, however illogical that may seem. Nazis, for example, toyed with the very non-German Breton nationalism. They did not get far.
2. But originally Etruscan. One Latin writer pinpoints their origin in the city of Vetulonia in what is now western Tuscany.

the first postwar years, but the mayhem in Russia, Lenin's autocracy, Stalinist tyranny and Europe's innate fears of barbarians coming from the east (they had been coming in waves for 2,000 years), together with communism's special threat to the propertied ruling classes, perpetuated an image of sanguinary apocalypse which fascists seemed better equipped than conservatives to combat. Frighteningly widespread economic failures and distress accentuated the divisions of societies into them and us and gave fascists the chance to make an appeal which traversed classes and the Left/Right stereotype. This appeal to material ill-being in conjunction with aggressive nationalism and general dissatisfaction with the ways of the modern world created mass movements with demagogic leaders. Fascist parties provided careers and a living as well as emotional outlets. Even then they were far from successful, particularly in countries with relatively stable political institutions and social systems. In France and Spain, Hungary and Yugoslavia, conservatives proved more adept at absorbing fascists than the other way round. In Romania the fascist Iron Guard achieved power for no more than a year before being pushed aside by Antonescu's dictatorship.[3] Only in Italy and Germany did the fascists successfully annex the forces of conservatism to fascism to win lasting control of the state.

Mussolini provided the outstanding example of fascist success in two basic respects: his regime lasted for twenty years, twice as long as Nazi rule in Germany, and it set the pattern. But it had also a peculiar advantage enjoyed by no other

3. Codreanu formed in 1927 the League which later became the Iron Guard. He was executed in 1938, the year after his party won third place in the Romanian parliament. The Iron Guard, which formed the government in 1940–41 after King Carol's abdication, was an ideological movement not unlike that of Ayatollah Khomeini in postwar Iran. It appealed on moral grounds to the young and poor, workers and peasants, teachers and priests – the broad scope characteristic of fascist attacks on a corrupt and back-sliding establishment. Its principal targets were the king, capitalism and all established political parties. Its attack on the bourgeoisie was comparatively light only because the Romanian bourgeoisie was insignificant, as too were the parties of the Left. It used power when it got it as violently and corruptly as previous regimes and so failed to inaugurate a moral renaissance. It had affinities with contemporary 'moral' crusades in Europe and with political movements which disfigured American public life later in the century.

fascist movement. In 1922 Italian fascism triumphed relatively easily over conservatives with the help of money from big business, sympathy from little men, a charismatic leader and – special to Italy – the most prestigious institution in the peninsula, the Vatican. After both World Wars the Vatican used its considerable influence to persuade the conservative Right and the fascist Right to make common cause against communism. It concluded with Mussolini in 1929 the first church-and-state agreement in Italy since the pope shut himself in the Vatican in 1870. Italy was a portent but also unique since the institutions of the Italian state co-existed with other institutions hostile to it and – however ramshackle financially and administratively – formidable and much older.

Mussolini's regime was rooted in war and destroyed by war. In both World Wars Italy joined in operations which would be disastrous for it unless they were short. In 1915 a profound division about whether to make war or not was won by those who were seduced by promises of postwar pelf, particularly by the promise of a share in imperial positions outside Europe. When Word War I unexpectedly lasted into 1919 the Italian economy was devastated. Its principal external resources – tourism and remittances from Italians working abroad – could not redress the deficit on its balance of payments. Public debt and inflation rose alarmingly. High taxes and prices ruined the small bourgeois and rural classes. Demobilised officers and men could find no work. All these victims of events railed helplessly against the small minority of profiteers and against the state which permitted them to flourish and had joined a war which had ended in a victory more bitter than exhilarating. The institutions of the state were discredited. There were strikes in cities, while in the countryside land-hungry peasants invaded private estates. The middling classes feared the proletariat and the peasantry, red revolution and civil war. Fascists were elected to parliament in 1919 for the first time. Gabriele D'Annunzio organised the seizure of Fiume by private enterprise in order to put the government to shame, while five postwar prime ministers displayed the feebleness of the authentic government. Mussolini was the sixth, summoned by the king to Rome where he arrived by train as, in some eyes, a saviour – a saviour with a sword or, more correctly, an axe and a bundle of rods.

Mussolini spurned ideas. The device on his banner was action which he elevated into a political principle. His aim was personal dictatorship. He suppressed political parties, freedom of the press and local government, but came to terms with the army in which – as in the royal family – he had a number of admirers. Political opponents believed that they could give him enough rope to hang himself, but, like Hitler's allies a decade later, they were wrong. He proceeded to subvert the constitution by law. In effect he substituted the Fascist Party and its derivatives, which were answerable and subservient to the Fascist Party, for the state under cover of establishing a new kind of corporatist state in which the corporations were organs of the fascist movement. Capital and labour were subordinated to party control and social problems were mothballed. People with problems such as poverty were put in prison. The ultimate sanction was not law, but fear and force, including murder.

Mussolini's interest in foreign affairs was at first low. Italy, like Germany, was a political creation of the nineteenth century. After unification, which meant above all the extrusion of Austria from the peninsula, and after the collapse of the Austrian and Russian empires, Italy played with the idea of replacing these extinct colossi as the dominant power in the Balkans. D'Annunzio's escapade was an offshoot of this delusion. Italy laid claim to Dalmatia and various Adriatic islands, but abandoned these claims when the nascent Yugoslavia agreed to allow Fiume to become a Free State (which Italy annexed in 1924). This concern for the Balkans stemmed less from the Fascist Party than the (aptly named) Nationalist Party of Luigi Federzoni, which was allied with the fascists until they absorbed it a year after coming to power. In his first years of power Mussolini was keener to achieve equality of esteem and prestige with the prime ministers of the leading European Powers than to challenge them. International intercourse and conferences were a means to arrive. The Locarno conference of 1925 gave him a seat at the top table and he was gratified by the approval of (in particular) British politicians, but Italy's claim to be one of Europe's regulators was always dubious and the Depression destroyed it. The economy was severely unsettled and the regime's tendency to intrigue and sleaze was aggravated, as too was its imperviousness to open and curative debate of its problems.

The Ethiopian war was a second disaster: expensive, irrelevant to current needs, without real or lasting popular support (unlike, in this respect, Hitler's widely popular campaign against the Versailles treaty) and welcome only to the army. The rejection in Britain and France of the Hoare–Laval plan to endorse Italy's unlawfully gotten gains cast Italy into Germany's embrace and deprived Mussolini of his coveted independence in foreign affairs. His intervention in the Spanish Civil War advertised his dependent partnership with Germany; the Pact of Steel of May 1939 vaunted this subordination; his hapless attempts at independent aggression in Albania and Greece exposed the unreality of his policies and earned him the ill-concealed irritation of his Germany ally. All these things weakened the fascist regime but did not remove it or make it less fascist. When in 1943 the western allies invaded Italy, the regime tried to survive without its Duce, who was deposed and imprisoned; and Italy was partitioned between Anglo-American and German forces until Germany's looming defeat beyond the Alps caused the surrender of the whole peninsula to the former. When the victors removed themselves, Italy reverted to democratic forms which were accepted by all parties from the extreme Right to the extreme Left. Fascists either had second thoughts about fascism or went underground or under other colours for the time being.

Italian fascism was never likely to cause a major war in Europe. Germany's fascists started a number of wars. German fascism – i.e. Nazism – was fashioned like Italian fascism by nationalism, economic setbacks and the talents of a remarkable leader. Both Germany and Italy derived a certain richness from the postponement until the nineteenth century of their unification as nation states. Although Italian nationalism was implicit in the development of the language used by Dante in the Middle Ages and likewise German nationalism in the name of the medieval 'Roman Empire of the German Nation' (called in English the Holy Roman Empire), the reality until the nineteenth century was a debilitating diversity. National unity, when achieved, was all the more vigorous and impetuous for its tardiness, partly in its opposition to the maturer nationalisms of neighbouring countries and partly because it coincided with the formidable forces of the industrial revolution, modern scientific education and modern technical efficiency. These spelled wealth and thence power, nowhere more so than in Germany where a German Reich sprang into being with the wealth and power which other Great Powers – France, Britain – had acquired only slowly over centuries. The German state covered in one bound the course from *anciens régimes* to modern state, the one represented by established conservative ruling classes, the other by far less conservative values. In France and Britain the rising industrial and financial classes displaced the landed aristocracy gradually and through the politics of partnership, easing themselves into political as well as economic power. In Germany, by contrast, the new middle and money classes, enthralled by the novelties of unity and national power, preferred to truckle to the traditional institutions which had fashioned this promising new Reich. Bismarck, Europe's most skilful politician in the nineteenth century, straddled and dominated the forces of monarchy, military and money, but after his deposition by Kaiser William II, Germany became a juggernaut drawn by wild visions in the souls of lesser men and precipitated two great wars and two great defeats for Germany. Defeat in the first of these wars was all the more searing for the power and pride which had gone before the fall and it rankled the more because victory had seemed close. The blame for defeat was laid on a supposedly craven home front as scapegoat and the terms of the peace settlement at Versailles were represented as monstrously vindictive and humiliating. These exaggerated reactions were crucially supplemented by two bouts of severe economic pain at the beginning and end of the 1920s. The second bout gave the Nazis a mass following and brought Hitler to power by election. Deflation and unemployment were disastrous for all but the Nazis. After a mere decade of democratic rule Germany turned back to autocracy which took the shape of Germany's old world Reich in fascist clothing. Hitler conquered the conservative classes before he overran the German state.[4]

4. The word 'guilt' did not appear in the famous war guilt clause of the Versailles treaty. The clause attached responsibility for the war to Germany, a milder reproof and a fair one. Reparations were heavy and foolish, but not out of the ordinary. The restrictions on German land and naval forces and the total ban on an air force were ultimately unenforceable and so more of an irritant than a hedge against renewed aggression.

Hitler, a more skilful politician than Mussolini who was an agitator and journalist turned politician, was not the shabby failed dabbler in hack art so often described, but a born leader, wily, resolute, efficient, who knew how to beguile big industrialists and small farmers (Germany was a land of both) as well as military and aristocratic elites and a mass audience. He was the most successful of all fascist leaders because he invaded the middle ground and held it for years. He was a German nationalist – German in the sense of the Germanic *Volk* – whose nationalism was more deeply rooted in Germany's ancient crusading venom against the Slav peoples than it was in the comparatively recent feuds with France over Franco-German borders or with Britain over sea power. Hitler's hatred and contempt for the Slavs, whom he proposed to kill and enslave, was racial with echoes of the peculiar bitterness which, characteristic of religious conflicts in general, had pervaded the first encounters between Christian Germans and pagan Slavs in the Middle Ages. Hitler gave this ancient clash a modern twist by his obsessive quest for living space for the expanding German people at the expense of the genetically inferior Slavs.

But first he had to find a champion who could unite and lead the Germans and he did not take long to do so: he appointed himself. By an amalgam of popular persuasion and brute force, he won control of the mind of Germany and the German state. He exploited, the more easily because he shared, popular indignation against Versailles and popular contempt for the flabby failures of postwar democratic governments. He destroyed the constitution by using it up to a point and then ignoring it. He seduced leading politicians of the Right, industrialists and bankers and generals who thought mistakenly that they were cleverer than he was. He won the game of conservatives versus fascists. He took about two years to transform the state: subverting and subordinating the judiciary, appropriating or cowing the press, cowing the churches, extinguishing political parties and labour unions, turning education into a branch of propaganda and generally terrorising all but the very boldest of his opponents. Since he never argued he was never openly faulted. Leadership meant assertion plus acquiescence and obedience; rational discourse and dissent were excluded, derided and punished. His pragmatism caused him, as it caused Mussolini, to maintain the regular armed forces instead of supplanting them by his private army (the SA) until the savaging of the army in Russia persuaded him to raise on the basis of the SS a new army (the Waffen SS) which was largely non-German: Napoleon had had to do the same in his latter years. The Jews, whom he hated at least as much as the Slavs and regarded as inhuman, he persecuted and mulcted until war enabled him to construct in Poland vast slaughterhouses to which German and other European Jews were transported in their millions to be killed.

But he lost the war. By 1945 Hitler was even more comprehensively beaten than Ludendorff in 1917–18. He was beaten by superior power, resources and organisation – by material things. Collaterally fascism was greatly discredited by the defeat in war of Europe's two pre-eminent fascist states, defeated in their own element. This was one of the most significant victories in the history of modern Europe, for without it the great power of Germany would have been at the service of fascist ideas and practices throughout Europe. But ideas, although they may be discredited, are rarely wiped out. Survival is their prerogative. Fascist ideas may fluctuate in intensity, but they remain in being and ready to revive when circumstances – and a sufficient interval for recuperation – favour them. After a shattering defeat like that of 1945 the place to look for their revival is not necessarily the scene of their recent triumphs and disasters. Democratic and ex-communist environments could be more propitious for them.

. . .

II

Since 1945 Germany and Italy have pointed in different directions. In Germany the catastrophe was so complete that a new state had to be constructed, equipped with a constitution and a Constitutional Court which banned fascist parties. For some years political parties and groups in West Germany concentrated on the plight of war victims (in, for example, the *Bund der Heimatlosen*). The mood was not only anti-fascist, but generally anti-nationalist. Right-wing parties received little support and steered clear of Nazi connections and slogans; they posed no threat to the Christian Democrats (CDU) who, led by the astute Konrad Adenauer, benefited from the country's unexpectedly swift recovery and exceptional prosperity. From the late 1980s, when the economy began to falter under the strains of unification with eastern Germany and worldwide recession, the CDU lost some of its gloss and nasty signs appeared in hostility to foreign workers, asylum seekers and Jews; Turkish workers, many of them now permanently resident in Germany, were killed. But there was no serious threat to democracy and no more than a warning to Germany's new found commitment to international good behaviour and to internationalism in preference to the pursuit of hegemonial world power. The German economy and the German government were robust enough to contain and minimise ugly reminders of the Nazi past. In Italy they were not.

Italy's devastation by war was far less than Germany's, but its humiliation was comparable, its exit from the war untidy and confusing and its recovery less spectacular. The United States, like the Vatican, was anxious to see a powerful consolidated right-wing regime as a bulwark against communism. Democratic forms were established and so long as the Cold War lasted the Democratic Christian Party ruled the roost, albeit with diminishing credit. In forming coalition governments it found partners among minor parties of the Centre and the Left rather than the extreme Right. *Uomo Qualunque*, a newspaper which developed into a party and a precursor of Pierre Poujade's party of the little man in France, represented one disgruntled section but made no lasting impression. More explicitly fascist was the Movimiento Sociale Italiano (MSI) which, with its strength mainly in the resentfully under-privileged south, remained in the wings trying to sort out internal dissensions. With the end of the Cold War the Democratic Christian Party's perpetual dominance lost its *raison d'être*; it and other established parties were exposed to damning charges of wholesale corruption; and a new right-wing coalition was fashioned by Silvio Berlusconi's *Forza Italia* (newspapers and other media transformed into a political party) with the Northern League (an assortment of decentralisers) and the MSI which changed itself into the

Aleanza Nazionale (AN) in an attempt to dilute or eradicate its fascist pedigree. This new constellation proclaimed its opposition to corruption and tried to distance itself from the Mafia and, more politely, from the Vatican. It did not last long. Of its discordant elements the AN had a more durable air than its partners.

Unlike Germany, Italy had neither a strong economy nor strong government and in this environment shadowy groups, military and clerical and the generally dissatisfied (the P2 Lodge for example), indulged in conspiracy and violence which erupted in fewer outrages than the equivalent left-wing activities, but killed more people. But democratic forms and political parlance survived. They did so too in Spain in 1981 when a right-wing coup was foiled. In Greece, however, a group of right-wing colonels whose ideas, so far as they had any, were more anti-democratic than fascist, seized power in 1967 and held it for seven years.

The principal democracies of western Europe regarded themselves as immune from such antics and from fascist infection. Were they too complacent? Their record was good but what made it so?

Charles de Gaulle is not only the outstanding figure in twentieth-century France. He epitomises it. He was by temperament autocratic, but he was also democratic. He exercised power autocratically, but held it democratically. When he did not get his way he departed the scene. He was not one of those who, like for example Margaret Thatcher, were determined never to retire or allow anybody to take his place. Between the wars France suffered many of the same ills as Italy without succumbing to fascism. The shocks and damage of World War I, which was fought mainly in France, were followed by economic calamity and political instability which shook the nerves of thousands and were blamed on the state and the existing order. These discords were brought to a half-close by the electoral victory of the conservative Right in 1926. The franc was stabilised – which is to say that it was prevented from falling any further – and in economic affairs France gained a respite of a few years before the coming of the Depression. This respite enabled the (largely non-political) middle to hold through the Depression and through the second bout of helplessness which the Depression engendered. It held again in spite of defeat in 1940 and Vichy. In this perspective the 1920s were crucial, but in a longer perspective what was crucial was the length and depth of the democratic tradition reaching back to 1789. Over the years and decades after the Revolution democracy lost some battles and won more, so that it came to be adopted as part of France's eternal heritage. France's democratic institutions and habits proved strong enough to withstand the buffets of material ill-fortune in peace and war and the lures of communism and fascism. But the war itself was at best an ambiguous experience. In Vichy, France had a home-grown fascist or quasi-fascist government which was not quite a German satellite nor an independent nation state.

Wars sharpen nationalism and will do so for as long as they are fought between states which call themselves and think of themselves as nation states. Napoleon's wars are commonly cited as the fashioners of modern European combative nationalism and even the Hundred Years War appears in books about the origins of French and English nationalism. World War II, in which state after state failed the essential task of defending its borders and citizens, devalued the virtually axiomatic belief in the nation state but, reactively, also sharpened nationalist loyalties which were under threat. In western Europe a postwar current set in towards closer and more permanent associations of states, beginning with the Coal and Steel Community and leading to the European Union – a trend which was for years overlaid and obscured by the Cold War. As this trend developed it evoked a nationalist reaction which had its nasty aspects and these aspects were accentuated when the economic climate deteriorated. From the 1970s healthy economies became less healthy and less stable, so that where anti-communism plus economic recession had presented opportunities to fascism between the wars, now economic recession plus internationalism did so once more. Internationalism threatened established identities. Economic perplexity threatened living standards, including in particular those of the little man caught between big business and big government on the one hand and a numerous and carping proletariat on the other. Both threats were xenophobic; both offered scapegoats in (usually coloured) immigrants and asylum seekers or in foreign bureaucrats; both egged on politicians who pandered to emotional prejudices with minimal regard to facts or consequences. Here was familiar and promising ground for fascists.

The most successful demagogue of the extreme Right in western Europe was Jean-Marie Le Pen. Not a charismatic figure in the class of Mussolini or Hitler, Le Pen was nevertheless an exceptionally good speaker capable of combining emotional and suggestive demagogy with simple and direct language. His message was often convoluted, but his manner was straightforward. He entered the French parliament in 1956 at the age of twenty-eight as a follower of Pierre Poujade's Union for the Defence of Shopkeepers and Artisans – the defender of the little man, meaning the independent little man rather than the industrial or rural wage-slave traditionally embraced by the Left. Poujadism was anti-capitalist, anti-establishment and anti-Semitic. Its heyday was in the mid-1950s and short. Its favourite issues were overshadowed by the Algerian crisis which entailed the return of de Gaulle, the creation of the Fifth Republic and the subordination for ten years of much political activity to de Gaulle's renewed charisma. Soon after de Gaulle's final departure Le Pen founded (1972) the National Front as a constitutional party to contest elections in a democratic manner and in 1984 he stood successfully for election to the parliament of the European Community. He normally abstained from anti-Semitic language but his main targets, from Pierre Mendès-France onwards, were Jews. As the name of his party proclaimed, his central theme was nationalism, for which France was fertile ground owing to its loss of empire, the need to keep up with a reconstructed Germany, the sacrifices of sovereignty to the EC/EU and the economic pains of the 1970s and beyond. The 1970s were also a peculiar time for France since, in addition to economic and national distractions, the French were uncertain about what France could or should be without de Gaulle and without a clear status in the European political system. De Gaulle was in retrospect a puzzling figure: a patriot beyond dispute but also a demonstrative friend of the new Germany and the European Community. Because de Gaulle had eclipsed politics, post-Gaullist France was a whirlpool in which mavericks like Le Pen could flail and flourish. In calmer waters he might fare less well but whenever French men and women feared foreigners competing for their jobs and dipping into the welfare pool somebody like Le Pen would be on hand to represent these fears and other latent prejudices.

The First Person in the French Revolutionary Trinity was *Liberté*. Freedom is at the core of the word *République* as surely as its opposite, the axe in the *fasces*, is at the core of fascism. In English, republican means no king, but in French, as in Latin, it means the state which, after the Revolution, was conceived as constitutional and democratic, however deviously these terms might be construed. This principle, although buffeted from time to time from Napoleon to Vichy, has been affirmed and consecrated. It has not, however, become wholly or permanently immune to anti-libertarian reactions such as these exemplified by Le Pen.

British democracy was even better entrenched. There has never been a realistic prospect of a British fascist party supplanting the Conservative Party, nor has the extreme Right had anything but marginal influence within it. The failures of Oswald Mosley, an intelligent and electrifying politician, tell a tale. A two-party system, which the British system nearly is, makes for large parties covering a broad political spectrum and embracing therefore a right-wing which tries to win friends and allies in the party's middling mass. A British Poujade or Le Pen with a party of his own is never more than a tactical bid to capture the Conservative Party by seceding from it in order to return.[5]

Between the wars the British Conservative Party, although far from fascist, included admirers of the fascist dictators and King Edward VIII was not only sympathetic to the Nazis,

---

5. I evade the question how far Britain is a democracy. It is more a democracy than anything else, but it may plausibly be labelled an oligarchy tending towards democracy. Its political stability derives from process rather than definition, from the adaptability of oligarchic forms slowly accommodating democratic ideas and rules. Its rhetoric and some of its institutions are democratic, but its values and habits remain significantly oligarchic. One of Winston Churchill's peculiarities, which was extremely important in his war leadership, was that he was markedly more democratic and devoted to parliament than much of the ruling class. As an aristocrat he could afford to be. His successors were either fake aristocrats or champions of the more insecure middle classes against the dreaded proles.

but may have tried to interfere unconstitutionally in foreign affairs (although he could have been moved by a genuine desire to prevent or, once it had started, stop an appalling war). Most significant, however, is the ease with which the Conservative government, having resolved to dethrone the king, did so, however adventitiously aided it was by the king's infatuation with an undesirable person.

After World War II the two-party system resumed its sway, but Britain was not wholly exempt from temptations. Postwar elation was followed by post-imperial malaise; the Rhodesian problem was more protracted than France's Algerian problem; Northern Ireland was even more protracted and much nearer home. European federalism, about which the British were content to remain ignorant until they became apprehensive, inflamed national nerves and the mismanagement of the economy by a series of (mainly Conservative) administrations further exacerbated xenophobia as jobs became scarce and foreign (mainly coloured) immigrants were blamed for taking the jobs or battening on social services. The fascist National Front, created in 1967, anti-Semitic as well as anti-black, focused these emotions but had little electoral success and was sidelined after the Conservatives regained power in 1979 with a right-wing leader in Margaret Thatcher.

Thatcher was a leader of uncommon vigour and directness, but more modest intelligence. Her talents were for combat, her instincts were narrowly nationalist and her temper was authoritarian. She belittled and emasculated local government; aimed to destroy rather than restrain or reform trade unions;[6] undermined the cabinet system by manipulating its committees; handled European issues with doubtful constitutional propriety; and took no trouble to disguise her disdain of foreigners, including the Commonwealth.

6. So too, whether Thatcher knew it or not, did Hitler and Mussolini. The vilification of unions was one of the more popular items in the dictators' prewar speeches and programmes, at least as popular in my recollection as Hitler's anti-Semitism or Mussolini's imperialism. A keyword in Thatcherite economic policies was productivity, which was a polite term for sacking workers. It made particular companies more profitable in the short run and eradicated lax over-staffing, but overall it damaged the economy by promoting stagnation rather than growth and revived memories of interwar unemployment and civil strife which had provided votes for fascists in many countries.

After her fall some of her followers went even further in their carelessness of the law and of the role of the judiciary.[7] These trends in British political life were all the more remarkable since there was in Britain no communist threat such as inspired and served to justify fascists on the continent. But, once again, the outstanding point was the resolve of the Conservatives in the House of Commons to remove Thatcher as summarily as Baldwin had removed Edward VIII. They did so partly because they feared for their seats and careers if they were to be required to fight an election with her as leader, but also because some of them had concluded that she had become dangerous.

The fascist threat to democratic western Europe at the end of the century seems small and remote, if not entirely negligible. The threat in ex-communist countries was neither negligible nor remote. The overthrow of communist rule brought freedom but not material ease or even material improvement. It also released nationalism.

The experience of eastern Europe after World War II was the reverse of what occurred in western Europe. In Stalin's satellite empire countries had been homogenised against their will and the dissolution of that empire released them into a pre-Soviet world with all that world's ancient divisions. Just when western Europe was experimenting with a new internationalism which diminished national sovereignties, eastern Europe was rejoicing in nationalism reanimated. These were old states restored and they did not emerge from Soviet rule with their old enmities washed away. They formed various mildly cooperative organisations (as they had done after World War I), but they had no great wish to unite; they wanted to be themselves once more. In Yugoslavia, not a Soviet fief but a multi-ethnic multi-religion federation invented after World War I and redesigned after

---

7. They were not necessarily fascist in intent but they stole fascist clothes and used slogans about public order and national identity in order to encroach on civic rights and repress or expel persons on grounds of their affinities rather than their acts. These were tell-tale signs. The Conservative Party had had members on whom the fascist label might be stuck but Conservative cabinets had not been open to them. Now they contained ministers from the party's far Right and others who found it expedient to pretend to have one foot in a fellow-travelling platoon.

World War II, the federal communist overlay was broken by rampant nationalisms.[8]

Russia, the largest and most powerful fragment of the dissolved Soviet Union, has never been a liberal or conservative or socialist democracy and there is little reason to suppose that it will become any one of these things at all soon. It may revert to Stalinist communism or to some milder form of communism although, if it does so, the cause will be disappointment with the new rather than love of the old order. There are elements of fascism in Russia. Whether they gain or lose in strength will depend on the ups and downs of the economy and the force of nationalism. Nationalism has been generated by the fall from great power, the recreation of a specifically Russian state, confusion over Russia's power rating in the world, its ambiguous relations with its internal ethnic minorities (searingly exemplified in Chechnya) and the appearance of figures such as the ultra

8. The Balkans should be distinguished from other parts of eastern Europe. The barbarous expression of ethnic/religious conflicts in and around Bosnia are only one face of a tragedy which has to be read back into the eighteenth century or earlier. In that period a small number of *savants* was attracted by western European thought which, most eminently represented by Descartes, Galileo and Newton, stood medieval thinking on its head and in addition challenged the revived Aristotelianism of the Renaissance. This intellectual revolution was followed by the Enlightenment which, particularly in the works of Diderot and Voltaire, penetrated tentatively into the Balkans where, however, the *savants* who welcomed it were few, suspect theologically, maligned and ultimately defeated. Their chief centres were Bucharest and Vienna, their language Greek, their cultural envelope Orthodox Christianity. Their prospect included, besides a general intellectual and pedagogic revolution, a Balkan Republic (minus the Ottomans). See P.M. Kitromilides, *The Enlightenment as Social Criticism* (Princeton 1992). This episode is symptomatic. Eastern (Orthodox) Christianity had already shrugged off a movement analogous to the Reformation in the west. By vanquishing the Enlightenment it further asserted the primacy of Authority over Conscience and Reason at a time when western Europe was at least acknowledging the tensions between these protagonists of freedom and, on the other hand, the demands of dogmatic authority. In the nineteenth century Orthodoxy compromised its claim to universalism and its eirenic role when, assuming a leading part in the struggle against the Turks, it split into a number of separate autocephalous churches on a national pattern and so abetted in the post-Ottoman Balkans a continuing warrior culture within which each nation state has sought aggrandisement at the expense of its neighbours.

nationalist Vladimir Zhirinowski. Zhirinowski may be a transient figure, just a clown, but if he is a clown he will be replaced by somebody who is not a clown. Economic morasses have not been cleared as quickly as many people in and beyond Russia hoped in the bright dawn of *glasnost* and *perestroika*. The notion that Russia might make a more or less peaceful transition to a liberal economy was grounded in a massive underestimate of the complexities of such a transition and of the funds required – or available – from the capitalist world to inaugurate and sustain it. The history of Russia in the twentieth century has been one of great disasters and, unlike Germany, Russia has few levers with which to entice friendship from rich and powerful strangers. It is in a state of uncertainty and apprehension and incipient anarchy comparable with the years from 1917 to the death of Lenin. A fascist leader could be a ready answer to wounded nationalism. In the presidential elections of 1996 Gennady Zuganov's campaign sounded more nationalist than communist.

A survey of European fascism should not ignore the United States of America. The Americans were pressed into Europe's wars in order to defeat the fascist dictators and were then co-opted into the European system in order to wage the Cold War. The United States influences Europe not only because it is the most powerful and most productive state in the world, but additionally because it has for fifty years been treated by Europe as a necessary factor in Europe's affairs. It has an exceptionally democratic tradition, but it makes flagwagging a pious duty, its central institutions are not widely trusted and it spawns with distressing ease national, religious and pseudo-ethical movements as illiberal as anything which the maddest mullah or rabbi might devise. It has immense resources and skills, but has contrived to choose as president a sequence of men to rival the worst dreams of a hereditary system in biological decline. Throughout the present century the American economy has been the symbol of American success and confidence, but it is no longer so assured and its very successes have contributed to the recklessness of leaders who paid for the Cold War and the Vietnam War by borrowing and the Gulf War by begging. Economic setbacks and disappointments where they are least expected may fertilise the dark side of charismatic politics, fundamentalist clerics and the aggressive impatience characteristic of frustrated giants – and of fascists of any stature.

. . .

III

Great wars beget great illusions. The most dangerous of the illusions begotten of World War II would be to suppose that fascism had been expunged. The Anglo-American democracies won the war, but not because they were democracies. Without belittling the inherent strengths and virtues of a democratic system and mentality, it has to be remembered that most European democracies were losers in World War II and that the Soviet contribution to the defeat of Germany made nonsense of any attempt to celebrate 1945 as the defeat of fascism by superior political virtue. Fascism survived, not in very good health but not terminally ill.

Fascism is not new. It is not an emanation of the present century and not likely to pass away with it. It has taken forms which derive from the modern demographic and industrial revolutions, from the age of the masses and the age of industrial weaponry, but its roots go deeper. The masses and the weaponry are the instruments with which it confronts changes which it seeks to reverse with an instinctive conviction that its ends justify any means. The revolt against change is a perennial feature of any civilisation which countenances change: the more profound the change the more ferocious the revolt. There are limits to the ability of people to assimilate change and the pace of change. *L'homme moyen intellectuel* refuses to be hustled into new ways and in the last four to five centuries of western civilisation he has felt hustled in a way which distinguishes modern times from the medieval age. In Europe's Middle Ages the disturbing impact of new and shocking ideas was cushioned by the slower tempo of the times as well as by deliberate and authoritarian repression (including in extreme cases death at the stake and a promise of eternal damnation), so that the forces of intellectual surmise and demonstration were, when not roughly extinguished, dispersed through time. In more recent times, as authoritarian battlements have been weakened, many new ideas and new norms have taken effect with more disconcerting speed. It is characteristic of the modern age, as it was not of the medieval centuries, that new ideas became too hard to bear so that the modern age engendered a violent and vicious reaction by ideological defences. In this process the validity of the new ideas and the validity of the reactive defences are not the main issue. The essential element is the working of the human mind as it may be modified by education on the one hand or propaganda on the other – by brain-training or brain-washing. To suppose that this situation will change is to suppose something of which there is neither sign nor rational expectation.

Finally and most disturbingly, fascism – whatever and wherever the negative preconditions for its flourishing – possesses one indubitably powerful positive appeal. Nobody doubts that it provides leadership. Whether democracy does so is doubted. World War II exemplified the resilience, underlying strength and inventiveness of democratic societies but it no less clearly demonstrated an ambivalent distrust of forthright leaders by making them appear acceptable only in times of crisis (it might be called the Cincinnatus syndrome). One of the lasting successes of fascism between the wars was to call in question the very notion of democratic leadership. Unhappily the postwar years have done little to dispel this dilemma, not only in Europe – Germany, so far, the healthiest exception – but also in the United States where the record of the presidency and of democratic politics in general has been an abject decline into incompetence. One result is the privatisation of politics – a grotesque contradiction – as political parties are treated with increasing apathy and consigned to a special political class which exists for no other purpose than to be blamed when things go wrong. That was what happened in Weimar Germany and it is the Achilles' heel of democracy. So long as leadership in a democracy means soft or mediocre leadership, fascists hold a trump card, for people want leadership. They want leaders who are difficult to find: strong but not authoritarian or dogmatic.[9] When they are offered a choice between authoritarian fascists and flaccid democrats they are as likely to choose the former as the latter.

9. Dogma rots the brain. It provides ready-made general answers in advance of particular circumstances. It is therefore an alternative to thinking.

Chapter 7

THE GERMAN QUESTION

. . .

I

The German Question is this: How can a powerful Germany fit into a European states system? Are the two compatible? After some 200 years that question has been altered to this: Can a powerful Germany fit easily or peacefully into any European system? Would a federal system accommodate the problem more easily than a states system? This is not, however, a shift in the substance of the question. A federal system might make it easier to handle the question by altering its modalities but the substance – the imbalance of power between Germany and its neighbours – remains. German power exists independently of the European system, be it a states system or a federal union.

The Germans have displayed a special capacity for surprising and alarming Europe. The rise to power of Prussia in the eighteenth century was swift and shocking. So too was the formation of the German state in the nineteenth. This state possessed two special features, both of them disturbing. It was in the middle of Europe and its nature was ambiguous. It was – essentially, if not completely – the Germans' nation state and it was also a Reich. The term Reich referred back to the Holy Roman Empire and forward to the Nazi Third Reich.[1] After the collapse of the Nazi Reich the Germans again surprised Europe by the swiftness of their recovery

---

1. *Das Dritte Reich* was the title of a book by the Conservative writer and polemicist Möller van den Bruck. It was published in 1923, the year before Hitler began writing *Mein Kampf* in prison.

and their return to a position of dominance in Europe. In World War II the anti-German allies fought to curb the power of Germany but did not do so for long. Germany without Hitler is not a weakened Germany. But it may be a significantly different Germany if the horrors and collapse of the Third Reich have changed the German mentality – as to which only time will conclusively tell. Speculation is hazardous but it is also a duty and it may be made less opaque by an infusion of history into the business of thinking about the future.

One of the most peculiar and salient features of European history is the break-up of the Latin language but not the German. The ancient Romans ventured across the Rhine into German territory and famously got a bloody nose at the hands of Hermann the German at the Battle of the Teutoburgerwald in AD 9. The Rhine became a frontier. Centuries later, after the Roman empire in the west had crumbled away, the Franks on the one side of the Rhine and then the Saxons on the other tried to re-create the empire. The Franks did so partly at the invitation of the new power in Rome, the papacy, rival successor to imperial Rome. The pope crowned Charlemagne emperor but Charlemagne's empire barely outlived him and as more centuries passed the Latin world fragmented into separate secular states going their separate ways, speaking different new languages and having, until the advent of Napoleon, no serious prospect of re-creating the Roman or any other empire.

But Europe never forgot the Roman empire and it survived in more than memory. Its ghost took up residence among the Germans and became the Roman Empire of the German Nation (*Römisches Reich der Deutschen Nation* – in English, the Holy Roman Empire: this title was conferred on it only in the fifteenth century). It was not an empire except in name; no emperor ruled in Rome and few went there; it was a loose conglomeration of hundreds of sovereign entities which accorded a ceremonial pre-eminence to an emperor provided he were a German and went through a form of election by a select few German princes.[2] This arrangement

2. Non-Germans were not always put off from vying for this insubstantial title. Aspirants included Henry III's brother, Richard of Cornwall, and Henry VIII himself. From the later Middle Ages the title was virtually

undermined the power of the German-speaking world in two ways. It acknowledged the existence of an emperor, but reduced him to an iconic phantom who evolved into a dynast who was normally at odds or at war with other German dynasts, and it retarded by centuries the consolidation of the German world into a coherent secular state. At the date of the French Revolution there were still more than 400 German states and the post-Napoleonic settlement reduced them only to forty. Nobody before Hitler reduced the number to one, not even Bismarck (who recoiled from pitting Hohenzollerns against Habsburgs).

Nevertheless the mere existence of the Holy Roman Empire contributed to the notion of a single German nation state (like France or England) and this notion was further strengthened when secular princes and religious reformers joined forces at the Reformation to reduce or abolish the powers of the pope for their several secular or spiritual purposes. In the sixteenth century Germans were becoming something more than a geographical expression or linguistic category. They were beginning to think of themselves as a people who ought to have a state.

Then came Prussia. Prussia evolved out of a loose confederation of assorted possessions of a branch of the south German family of Hohenzollern which, by chance, had added the militant eastern outpost of Prussia to its electorate of Brandenburg around Berlin. This conglomeration resembled the Papal States of central Italy rather than the consolidated monarchies of western Europe, but in an astonishingly short time it was fashioned into a state of the middle rank and then a European Great Power. In the hundred years (1640–1740) between the accession of the Great Elector of Brandenburg and that of his great-grandson King Frederick of Prussia these Hohenzollern territories were federated into

---

the property of the Habsburgs and, after the death in 1740 of Charles VI without a son, of the House of Lorraine, beginning with Charles VI's son-in-law and ending with Francis II who became instead Emperor of Austria: partly in deference to Napoleon and partly because there was no longer a secure Catholic majority among the Electors. The Habsburg dynasty, kings of Hungary after 1526 as well as dukes of Austria etc., found its destiny in defending Europe against the Turks and did not survive the end of the Ottoman empire.

a military and, by the standards of the times, tightly organised and efficient state. The Great Elector, who had a half-Dutch mother and a Dutch wife, treated ruling as a profession and was not above getting his hands dirty. He busied himself with a whole range of unprincely details (like Tsar Peter the Great), trebled his income, ruled for nearly fifty years and turned Brandenburg-Prussia into a strictly regulated workplace where the civil administration and even the clergy were obliged to fulfil work quotas and observe timetables and the country's resources were devoted first, foremost and almost exclusively to the creation of an army better organised and trained than any seen in Europe since the days of the Roman legions: an image which, later transferred to Germany as a whole, stuck in the minds of Germans and non-Germans for two centuries and more.

This Prussia was far from being an agreeable place to live in, even for generals and ministers, still less for the lower orders, but it was the first modern state which even tried to keep proper accounts, established primary education for all from five to thirteen, and broke the European mould of the state as a field of tension between crown and nobility by turning the landed aristocracy into a military caste allied with the monarchy instead of a congenitally discontented baronage trying to cramp the monarch's style. Frederick the Great used the position which he inherited from his forebears with audacity, military and political skill, brazen faithlessness and conspicuous, if temporary, success. He invaded and annexed part of the Austrian dominions; made Prussia a Power in Europe as well as Germany; and stoked a vigorous self-confidence which nurtured the belief that God was on Prussia's side – or was lucky to have Prussia on his side. Yet there was something manic about Prussia and its rulers. Frederick's father was obsessive to the verge of dementia and Frederick himself was a brittle mixture of energy in overdrive, total lack of principle and at the same time a devotee of the Enlightenment. Prussia in the eighteenth century was a state so concentrated on its military performance that it neglected, even shackled, its commercial and industrial classes and opportunities and, less surprisingly, showed not the slightest trace of any incipient democratic awareness. Yet this was the beginning of the industrial revolution, the eve of the democratic revolution and the age of Germany's emergence as an intellectual and artistic force second to none in Europe.[3]

After Frederick's death Prussia's fortunes faltered but were adventitiously revived, dashed and revived again by Napoleon who destroyed the old ramshackle German system, reduced the number of German states to forty, abolished the Holy Roman Empire and fashioned a new tripartite pattern consisting of Austria, Prussia and a confederation of all the rest. He also contributed unwittingly to the growth of a German identity by annexing parts of Germany to France, making the rulers of Bavaria and Württemberg kings but therewith French satellites, and inflicting crushing defeats on Germany's two Great Powers, Austria and Prussia, in successive years. In 1813 he was defeated by (largely German) forces in the great *Völkerschlacht* at Leipzig, the Battle of the Nations. His Russian campaign of 1812 was the beginning of his end, Waterloo the *coup de grâce*; but the Battle of Leipzig was the centrepiece of his downfall and the evaporation of his empire.

The Congress of Vienna adopted the Napoleonic pattern for Germany with modifications and so set the stage for the contest between Austria and Prussia which was to be the principal theme of the new century. Austria was given the permanent presidency of a German federation but in the new world of the nineteenth century Austria suffered two serious disabilities: it was not a state but an old-fashioned family hereditament with an imperial crown attached; and Vienna at the far south-eastern edge of the German world was no place for a pan-German capital. It was a Reich but not a German Reich. At best, and if the German world was to be further refined into just two states, Austria would be the obvious leader of the southern half. But Germany was headed not for bisection but for near unity under Prussian

---

3. Especially in music from Schütz to Schoenberg but also in architecture from the Baroque to the Bauhaus and in poetry, philosophy, mathematics and the physical sciences: in the jargon of a later age, a centre of excellence. Frederick the Great, flautist and minor composer, provided Bach with the theme for one of his greatest works. Frederick's successor, Frederick William II, was a competent cellist and commissioned a set of six string quartets from Mozart: he got three.

leadership and by the exclusion of Austria and its multi-ethnic empire.[4]

At mid-century (1848) a clutch of abortive revolutions and still-born schemes for constitutional reform exposed the feebleness of German liberal democracy (still a foreign import or fad) but also revealed to the more percipient politicians the need to give the old order a new base. Bismarck did this in Prussia. He enlisted the industrial and financial middle classes and the burgeoning national spirit in the service of a state dominated by conservative landowners and a military caste under the aegis of the authoritarian Hohenzollern dynasty; and by way of a North German Federation (1867) and a new German Reich (1871) he created the nearest available entity to a German nation state. He chose that this state should stop short of the Austrian borders partly because a wider Germany would be less Prussian and partly because there was as yet no way of including Austria without its numerous non-German appendages. The new German Reich was therefore unstable, an over-mighty state with uncertain frontiers and a form of government distasteful to half Europe – a *tour de force* made possible by Bismarck's outstanding political skills and twenty-eight years of uninterrupted power over his state, his monarch and his own unstable temperament. After his dismissal in 1890 by Kaiser William II the next twenty-eight years saw five chancellors and the accentuation of this instability at the heart of Europe.

The rise of Prussia to pre-eminence in the German world was one of the most important events in the modern history of Europe, for it signalled the transfer of power in Europe from France to Germany which even Napoleon could not prevent. So long as Austria held the top place in the German world France was able to keep that world divided. For Austrians German unity meant the Holy Roman Empire: the Austrian archduke was Holy Roman Emperor until 1806 and thereafter a pale imitation of that phantom office. But Prussia united Germany or most of it as a modern secular state with nothing Holy or Roman about it and no other German states allowed (except the Habsburg hybrid on the

---

4. The Habsburgs were gradually forced into sharing power with the Hungarian nobility which, unlike the Prussian aristocracy, remained suspicious and hostile towards the crown.

fringe). Prussia/Germany outranked France economically and demographically and, unlike Austria, had as much right as France to call itself a nation state and exercise a leading role in the European states system.

A system of states may be ordered in either of two ways – by a balance of power or by the dominance of one of them over the rest, *Gleichgewicht oder Hegemonie*.[5] Both systems accept the principle that all states are equal in status, but operate on the basis that in politics power matters more than status. The one system recognises the special power of a few states, the other accepts willy nilly the special power of one: the first system is ordered by management, the second by command.

A balance of power requires an enduring capability to form an alliance sufficiently strong to deter or defeat a single power trying to assert hegemony; a fluidity and flexibility in and between the elements of the system in order to ensure, as a first priority, the survival of the system; a shared political culture which endorses these aims; and a class of managers called statesmen, who put the interests of their states first but treat the viability of the system as one of those interests. After 1871 it was widely feared that Germans did not accept a system of this kind for the conduct of international affairs but, on the contrary, preferred to go for *Hegemonie* – an over-lordship such as the Romans had achieved and Napoleon had attempted. This threat was familiar in a general way but, by 1871, also novel for it was fortified and transmitted by the application of the industrial revolution to warfare and the recruitment of the civilian population to militant nationalism.[6] The heightened fear of hegemonial pretensions was part of the problem, for it predisposed all major states to make plans and take steps which increased distrust and accelerated war. From the eighteenth century, if not earlier, the state was equipped primarily for war and between 1871 and 1914 war was an increasingly consuming topic of international discourse. Germany, although the most feared state and the one most frequently cast as warmonger, was

5. See Ludwig Dehio, *Gleichgewicht oder Hegemonie: Betrachtungen über ein Grundproblem der neueren Staatengeschichte* (Krefeld, 1948). English translation *Germany and World Politics in the Twentieth Century* (London, 1959).
6. It is common to bewail the fate of civilians involved in the miseries of modern war, but civilians have been among the most ferocious warmongers.

in many ways no different from its peers among the Great Powers. It was more powerful on land than any other, it occupied a geographically menacing position, it harboured expanionist ambitions in Europe and beyond (colonies, the Middle East) and it was less inhibited than others by the dangers of a game which all were playing. But it was animated by the same colonial, commercial and naval rivalries as other Powers and by the same fears of cabals against it, pre-emptive strikes and a breakdown of international order. In the immediate and critical prelude to war in 1914 Germany's actions were especially disastrous, notably in prodding Austria into the attack on Serbia which in military terms started the war. Germany was different, but not all that different. What then should be done with it in the hour of its defeat?

The winners in the Great War of 1914–18 had a number of aims to which they attached varying degrees of importance. They wanted certain territorial changes, partly to reverse the verdicts of previous wars and partly to strengthen their own strategic defences, and they wanted further to weaken Germany's capability to make war by disarming it and imposing swingeing financial punishment. Besides doing what they could to diminish Germany's power they hoped that the Germans would alter their mentality by substituting a more pacific democracy for their traditional autocratic militarism. This hope was, however, both vague and secondary and the peace terms imposed on Germany did less than nothing to promote it. Criticism of the Treaty of Versailles has been directed primarily at the harshness of its terms, but these were more foolish than outrageous and the treaty's main failing was its incompatibility with any plausible prospect of changing German minds and attitudes. The old regime had gone with the abdication of the Kaiser and the humiliation of the military, but the leaders of the new democracy, who were in much the same position as Talleyrand and the French at Vienna after Napoleon's abdication, were not invited to the peace conference nor were they allowed to discuss or comment on the terms of the treaty which was presented to them for signature: they were expected to attend at Versailles with pens, but not tongues. They were saddled with the acceptance of formal responsibility for all the damage done by the war by a clause which, inserted in the treaty in order to justify the exaction of maximum financial reparations, stoked German resentment in the next generation and became one of Hitler's most valuable tools on his road to seizing power and justifying another war. The treaty itself was much like other treaties, but the conference which produced it was a conference between the victors and not between the victors and the defeated. This was a diplomatic blunder and a psychological disaster. In Germany the republic created at Weimar in 1919 was, according to its makers, the most democratic democracy in the world but it was so unsure of itself that it chose an ancient field marshal from the Hohenzollern age as its president, did not last long and was succeeded by the most vicious tyranny in German history.

The space between the two wars was so short – twenty years – that these wars have been treated as two acts in a single drama. This is a misleading view. Hitler's war had a much more precise and premeditated source than the Kaiser's. As set out in *Mein Kampf* – a book so famous that it is always referred to by its German title[7] – Hitler proposed to make war in order to win for Germany territory to the east without which the German race would expire. This was a fantastic idea, but he held and proclaimed it and, further, identifying Bolshevism with international Jewry, he was able to combine his two principal motives: anti-Semitism and the conquest of *Lebensraum* for Germany from the Soviet Union. The planning and execution of the resulting wars was fortunately imperfect although, like Ludendorff in 1918, he came close to winning (in Russia in 1941 and in the Atlantic in 1942). Had he won he would have re-arranged Europe in accordance with two guiding principles: that politics is purely power in action and that the Germans were superior in virtue as well as power to every other nation or race. For him, therefore, Europe was once more a geographical expression to be divided between Germans and non-Germans as best suited the Germans. There would be a zone of German habitation (*Grossraum*) measured and delineated by the supposed needs of the German race, leaving the rest of Europe to be parcelled into subordinate habitats for inferior peoples serving the economic requirements of the German *Grossraum*. He had no use for balance of power systems. His system was a

7. It was published in Germany in two volumes in 1925 and 1926.

command system and not a management system. His German nationalism excluded equal status for other nations by virtue of the law of nature which had decreed Germans to be better than non-Germans. He was in his own eyes literally on top of the world – or at least of Europe.

None of this came about because when the war came the British refused to give in, the Russians fought back and the Americans came in; but when the war was over the victors had to bear in mind that the Third Reich's programme for Europe had had more than a little appeal for different sections of the German people. The victors also had in mind the failure of their predecessors of 1919 to find an answer to the German Question. These comparisons were nagging but also inexact, for Germany's situation in 1945 was not what it had been in 1919.

In World War II Germany was battered very severely and eventually invaded from all sides and completely subjugated. The Nazis had perpetrated atrocities incomparably more appalling than any in the first war and only a small minority refused to believe that this had been so. The revelation of these dreadful deeds made a profound mark, not least in Germany, so that after 1945 Germans had to confront not only defeat but also horror and dishonour: Germany's peculiar blend of high achievement and high culture with barbarity. On their side the victors were divided among themselves since the Russians, themselves defeated before the end of the first war, were massively triumphant at the end of the second after suffering horrific casualties and vicious cruelties on an immense scale. Retribution was the dominant note on their side but not, this time, on the western side. There was, therefore, no peace treaty with Germany and so no *Diktat* after the manner of the Paris peace conference; there was no attempt to re-arrange Europe until twelve years later; and within less than five years – and thanks to the Cold War – a democratic Federal German Republic had come into being as an ally in a western alliance and with the American aid which started it on the road to prosperity, respectability, confidence and stability. If national mentalities may be changed by dramatic events then the experience of Nazism and the unexpected sequel to the war might be expected to do more than any others in two centuries to change the mind of Germany.

The Federal Republic of (initially) western Germany excluded not merely Austria but much of Prussia, all Saxony, the Saar (briefly) and more besides, but it was as democratic as Weimar, far more blessed in its material fortunes and anything but unsure of itself. Forty years later it recovered the eastern lands which had been subjected to the Soviet Union. It was guided by a chancellor – Konard Adenauer – who was no less shrewd than Bismarck and displayed a much nicer blend of authority and parliamentary decorum.[8] He sought rehabilitation with twin policies of democracy at home and union in Europe, with which he scored in 1953 a triumphant electoral victory. His course was put at risk in the next year when France rejected a European Defence Community but de Gaulle's return to power in 1958 consolidated the Franco-German accord which had created the Coal and Steel Community and the EEC and became all but axiomatic with both statesmen's successors.

. . .

II

The Federal Republic has by now (1996) lasted five times as long as the Weimar Republic. It has achieved peacefully its prime aim of re-incorporating communist east Germany, has established effectively a (mainly) two-party political system in which the broad Right and the broad Left alternate or combine in government, has commanded the support of the German people, the German armed services and the lords of the German economy, has refrained from playing off east against west in the manner of prewar power politics, and has become the leading proponent of European collaboration and union. But it is rash to set too much store by changes in mentalities. The very term is vague; changes in the mind of a people are even more difficult to assess than changes in the mind of an individual; and they are unpredictably reversible. But changes do occur and changes

8. Adenauer's political career began in 1906. It was interrupted by the Nazis. Its resumption after 1945 recalls the case of the celebrated Spanish scholar who, having been dismissed from his post by Franco, returned to it after the dictator's death in 1975 with a lecture which he began with the words: 'As I was saying . . .'.

in circumstances, which are less difficult to observe, affect mentalities.

The German Question needs to be re-stated and re-examined in the light of changing circumstances. At its core are the European states system and the position of the Germans in it. The system was predicated upon the distribution of power between states which were arrayed against each other, judges of their own best interests and answerable to no higher authority for their actions. The position of Germany in the system was that of the most powerful of these states, exercising power by militarism in alliance with nationalism – two factors which have been axiomatically accepted for generations as necessary and proper attributes of the territorial state; and specially conditioned by Germany's geographical position in Europe – exposed to dangers and tempted by opportunities. It may therefore most pertinently be considered from three quarters: from the west, from the east and from Russia.

Germany today patently covets nothing in western Europe which could be considered worth fighting for: in reverse, western European fears of German aggression have become less pressing than jealousies of German successes.[9] From its first chancellor, Konrad Adenauer, the Federal Republic placed uncommonly close relations with France at the top of its international agenda and adopted unreservedly a policy of adopting, deepening and widening European union. There is no longer any question of the use of German military might to secure hegemony over all Europe in spite of western Europeans. Even in the 1930s Hitler's aim was military conquests in the east without having to fight in the west. (His big miscalculation was that the one turned out to be unachievable without the other.) Eastward the outlook is less clear and the further east the more unclear.

Throughout the nineteenth century and until the disappearance of the Ottoman empire the European Great Powers pursued in eastern Europe policies which were openly adversarial and frequently belligerent. With the extinction

---

9. Herein lies the main distinction between American and British attitudes to Germany. The Americans are not jealous of German success. They believe that they created it postwar. And they do not fear German competition for power in Europe or the world. There has been Anglo-German competition in both.

of the Ottoman empire and the coincidental extinction of the Tsarist and Habsburg empires there ensued a brief interlude when France and Germany jockeyed for primacy in the east and the Germans won, not through the use of force, but by superior economic power and the superior economic guidance of Dr Hjalmar Schacht. Hitler's failed invasion of the Soviet Union gave Stalin virtually uncontested control of much of this area, forfeiting only Greece to western sea power and Yugoslavia to indigenous communism. The end of the Cold War introduced no new overlord, but restored the variety of states which – together with the states which emerged from the simultaneous disintegration of the Yugoslav federation – were all eager to join the European Union partly in search of economic aid and partly as a guarantee against renewed Russian aggression. The salient fact of the period 1919–89 is that, whereas before it the Balkans excited hostility among major European Powers, after it the interests of these Powers began to coincide. They might disagree about how best to handle a crisis – they certainly did in Yugoslavia – but they had come to agree over the paramount need to ensure stability rather than seek to profit at one another's expense from instability. Territorial pickings were off the agenda and territorial and other disputes between and within the states of central Europe and the Balkans were henceforward plainly best handled in concert. For the first time ever the national interests of leading states coincided more than they diverged.[10]

Russia poses questions of a different order and could well cause rifts among Europe's leading states. Russia has scared or antagonised Europe mightily not only under Stalin but long before him. It could again become a major Power, and probably will. Its temper is peculiarly unpredictable, if only because its history has been so turbulent within its borders as well as beyond them. Its ethnic problems are as acute as they were in the 1920s and its economy worse. It remains

10. One may justly be cynical about the term vital national interests. Ostensibly it refers to security – security of the national territory and more recently the 'security' of jobs. In the first sense it has too often been used as a veneer for offensive rhodomontade or as cover for illegal adventures. In the latter sense it is a way of pointing an accusing finger at a foreign scapegoat for the unemployment caused by incompetent handling of the domestic economy.

heavily armed, if not at present an efficient military Power. It is economically chaotic, but has vast resources which modern technology will extract and bring to international markets sooner or later.

If – when – Ukraine and Belarus[11] rejoin Russia by some form of reintegration there will be serious territorial issues in central Europe, where Russia has for the time being no frontiers, and these issues will be of greater concern to Germany than to Europeans further west. In any debate over attitudes to Russia Germany will be in the European driving seat even more positively than in debates over anything else. There is, in short, a Russian Question but not the Russian Question of 1945 and the Cold War. The new Russian state will resemble the old Tsarist empire in its extent and pretensions rather than the sprawling Soviet empire which looked like the Tsarist empire but was in reality closer akin to the Habsburg empire, riddled with that empire's incoherence as well as fatal contradictions of its own. The monstrous Soviet empire was engaged by the United States on account of its worldwide pretensions and destroyed, but a revived Russian empire will be an element in a European system and not a protagonist in a bipolar world system. Much will depend on how Europeans, wisely led or insiduously pushed by Germany, confront the new Russia – and, in reverse, on the shape and temper of a new Russia, which are still undetermined. There will be divided counsels. Some will seek to keep Russia militarily and economically weak as the allies of 1919 sought to diminish Germany (the policy of turning an orange into a tangerine); others will argue for an accommodation such as the western allies of 1945 effected with Germany. And the United States will take part in the argument. The manifest danger is Russian nationalism with a cutting edge. Greater still would be the resurgence of nationalism in Russia and Germany at the same time. The victims would be in the lands between them – victims of either Russo-German

11. Belarus is to Russia what Austria was to Germany after 1919. It has many reasons for needing closer association with Russia, with which – unlike Ukraine – it has no substantial ethnic conflict. Most Russians, like most Germans after 1919, are little concerned about a reunion which they might welcome but do not need. But some Russians positively want reunion with Belarus as a counter to the eastward spread of NATO.

hostility or Russo-German amity as practised by Frederick and Catherine the Great and, briefly, by Hitler and Stalin in 1939–40.

These alarming possibilities presuppose the persistence of the European states system in something like its historical form, but that too is sensing change. Europeans love their states – at any rate in opposition to other states – but they have become uneasy about the state as an essentially combative unit and about a states system whose ultimate regulator is war. They are in two minds about the state: *vorrei e non vorrei*. There has been considerable disenchantment with the state but at the same time no tried alternative to it as guarantor of freedoms and director of progress. There is less concern with frontiers and territory and therefore smaller appetite for military competition; more concern with commercial and financial health and therefore with cooperation, even permanently institutionalised cooperation. In reality the state's military power has always rested on its economic resources but those who exercised the power were mostly landowners, lawyers, professional politicians – anything but economists; and the electorate, where it existed, has been persuaded with relative ease to endorse lavish and uneconomic military budgets or give tacit approval to waging wars on credit. Even in the relatively open democracy of the United States successive administrations were minded and allowed to wage war by borrowing, notably in Vietnam and the Gulf; and the Cold War, which ruined the Soviet Union, did great damage to the American economy, only partly masked by the fact that the damage to the Soviet economy was deadlier sooner. During the Cold War France and Britain too spent huge sums on nuclear weapons which could be of no use in war and were therefore much less of a deterrent than was commonly claimed. Germany by contrast (and Japan) became a greater power without such weapons.

The half century since the end of World War II has seen a growing perception that the central question about the exercise of power lies not in a comparative tally of armaments, but in the answers to two very different questions: how may economic power be exercised; and how does economic power affect political aims and policies? Frederick the Great inherited and deployed superior military force and won with it startling successes even though he neglected or mistook the needs of the Prussian economy. His contemporaries in Europe followed the same path with more or less success but none of their modern successors would conduct affairs of state so myopically. Consequently they are obliged to reckon that the powers of the state must be marshalled in different ways and for different purposes – above all, not on the battlefield in order to seize territory from another state; for if economic power is the supreme attribute of a state then war is a bad way of asserting it since war may destroy the winner's economy as much as the loser's. After turning all Europe into a battlefield Europeans have been absorbing that lesson and, however reluctantly, adapting their minds to it. The Germans have done so better than most.

Two defeats in two World Wars created exceptional circumstances and good fortune added exceptional men. Konrad Adenauer was followed by two other remarkable chancellors in Willy Brandt and Helmut Schmidt, while coincidentally in France the same generation produced Charles de Gaulle and Jean Monnet. These last two men were not unalloyed admirers of one another but they respected one another's talents and character and their calibre as statesmen. When exceptional times coincide with exceptional men it is permissible to speak of turning points in history and important not to miss them. Germany cannot be other than central and powerful and it has therefore choices. These choices are necessarily described in precise terms because description makes things precise in order to make them more intelligible, but in reality the choices are not between sharply contrasted policies but choices about how to combine them. In stark terms Germany might choose nationalism and a states system which it would dominate with the least interference from other states, or alternatively an uncompromising and radically new federal system. The balance of power system based on the sovereign state has not served Germany well, for although Germany became the greatest power in the system it lost the two great wars which the system engendered. The electors of Brandenburg declined (as Macaulay observed) to accept their inferiority to the electors of Saxony and Bavaria, and the Prussian kings and German emperors declined to accept their inferiority to anybody. Frederick the Great made Prussia a Great Power but he made few Prussians happy or prosperous and in World War II Germany suffered in a measure far surpassing what a corner of France suffered in the first war or England has suffered at any time in its history. Further, the record of the balance of power system in keeping the peace is at best dubious, while in economic matters the nation state is a contradiction in terms. Germany needs another system in which German power – economic before military – will reap full dividends. Moreover a reversion to the old system in its pristine shape is all but inconceivable. The European Union has put down tough roots, excited strong expectations and weathered testing storms, and although it may be attenuated in some parts and delayed in others, it will not be abandoned. The stark alternative to the resurrection of the states system is an emphatic strengthening of the Union but, again, this will be qualified to mean strengthening it in politically expedient ways and without pressing contentious aspects to the point of deadlock in the Council of Ministers. (The crux is not a single currency, which is a natural adjunct of a single market, but single foreign policies.) Some timetables will do what timetables usually do (there is a legal maxim which says that time is not normally of the essence of a contract). But Germany, which for fifty years has had an *Ostpolitik* as well as a Franco-German policy for western Europe, sees itself as a pivot or ligature with a European Union as its field of action. If this interpretation is correct then there is at least a good case for supposing that the disasters of this century have changed the mind of Germany radically; that there is a tide in the affairs of Europe which statesmen and others whose business it is to form working judgements about the future may not safely or wisely spurn; that the old German Question is dead – one of the few welcome casualties of World War II. The failure to arrive at a German peace treaty immediately after the war emerges in retrospect as a blessing in disguise. It enabled Germany to be re-absorbed into Europe and, with the Treaty of Rome in 1957, take its due part in re-ordering the continent. The Treaty of Rome was the true end to World War II in Europe and the hope of a new and more stable order which Versailles failed to provide. It was not Versailles II but Vienna II.

Chapter 8

THE COLD WAR AS CODA

. . .

I

World War II ended with the surrender of Germany and
Japan within a few months of one another. The verdict was
total and incontestable. Among the victors, two – the United
States of America and the USSR – were dubbed Superpowers. Yet fifty years later Germany and Japan were among
the most powerful states in the world; the USSR had ceased
to exist and even its largest component, Russia, was not a
Power of the first rank; the United States, although still pre-
eminent economically and militarily, was gravely damaged
and in some ways inferior to Japan; and China loomed.
President Clinton began his second term by proclaiming the
importance of American-Chinese accord in world affairs.

The decisiveness of victory obliterated for a while the fact
that the losers had come near to winning. Had Hitler won
either the Battle of Britain or the Battle of the Atlantic, two
close encounters, the Americans could not have landed huge
armies in Europe. Stalin held Moscow and Leningrad only
narrowly. Japan crippled the American fleet at Pearl Harbor
not quite enough and altogether demolished the British,
French and Dutch empires in East Asia before crashing to
defeat.

Customarily the immediate outward signs of a great war
are territorial changes, if only because wars are fought by
states which are defined by their boundaries and because
the turmoil of war helps peoples to assert claims to state-
hood. But after World War II boundary changes in Europe
were either few or masked. In western Europe changes were

159

limited to putting the losers back where they came from; in central and eastern Europe, changes – apart from the Russo-Polish borders – did not show on the map because six nominally sovereign states reduced to vassalage by the Soviet Union continued to be shown as independent instead of being coloured red: the formalities obscured the reality. Outside Europe, Italy, like Germany after World War II, was stripped of its African possessions as well as losing its fleeting five-year occupation of Ethiopia. There were in Europe no formal redistributions of territory comparable with those occasioned by the disintegration of the Tsarist, Habsburg and Ottoman empires. (But the outcome in eastern Asia and the Pacific after 1945 was analogous to that in Europe after 1919. Japan was forced to retreat not only from its recent conquests but also from Taiwan, Korea, its mandated Pacific islands and Manchuria, acquired in 1895, 1910, 1920 and 1931 respectively: amputations of almost Habsburg calamitousness.)

Paradoxically, however, at one remove from the war itself, European empires were dissolved by World War II – the empires of the winners. The war accelerated major changes which, although vaguely premeditated before the war, had been envisaged for the barely foreseeable future. Whereas the first war had dismantled empires in Europe, the second did the same for European empires in Asia and Africa. The restoration of Ethiopian independence, the retreat of the British from India, the failure of European Powers to re-establish themselves in South East Asia, and the experiences of Africans themselves in distant theatres of war contributed to insistent and sometimes belligerent demands for independence to which Britain, France and the Netherlands succumbed in Asia and then in Africa, followed in the latter by Belgium and eventually Portugal and Spain. Within a generation after the end of the war the number of independent states in the world was trebled. The event was not unforeseeable but its timing was all but universally unforeseen.

Besides being numerous, most of the new states were poor or very poor – poor in resources, education, skills, professional services and standards, experience in government and experience of the world. They expected to become less poor quickly, but most of them were afflicted by two comprehensive disadvantages: political instability and unprecedented population explosion. They started with high hopes and much goodwill but they failed to convert goodwill into material assistance on the scale which they hoped for or into the respect which they needed to preserve sympathy in the face of the corruption and incompetence of successive civilian and military regimes. Nevertheless the mere existence of these states changed the face of world affairs. Instead of being the preserves of a particular imperial Power, each became an open field for opportunity and opportunism and for the machinations and conflicting interests of many Powers, notably in relation to the Cold War but also generally in the competition for materials and markets. Tempted to play one outsider off against another, the new states did themselves little good in the process, insufficiently united among themselves and insufficiently powerful even where united. At the United Nations they changed the tone of international affairs and in some degree the agenda but not the substance.

The outstanding sequel to World War II was the Cold War. It lasted for most of the ensuing half century, nearly ten times the span of World War II. Its sources included cultural and ideological elements but it was primarily a contest about power and a consequence of miscalculations.[1] The protagonists – the United States and the USSR – feared one another. They also disliked, even hated, one another but without the fear there would have been no Cold War: coldness certainly but not war. Just as western Europeans never contemplated going to war against Hitler's Germany on account of his vices until German power became menacing, so the United States would never have assailed the USSR on account of its tyranny if it had not feared Soviet power.

There were fears on both sides and these fears were exaggerated. American fears rested on two false assumptions: first, that the Soviet armies might advance from Germany yet further westward and, secondly, that communist parties might seize power in France, Italy or elsewhere. Soviet victories over German armies in the last two years of the war gave the Soviet armies an awesome repute which concealed the prostration of the Soviet Union through enormous losses

1. Incomprehension is perennially powerful in international affairs. In *The Making of the Middle Ages* (London, 1953), Richard Southern pinpoints mutual incomprehension as the prime source of conflict between Western and Eastern Christendom which produced centuries of silly venom.

in human lives, the devastation of industrial and agricultural production and the ruin of the Soviet economy. The Soviet armies were able to maintain their grip in central and eastern Europe which they had already overrun and where they faced no opposition, but the notion that they might advance to the Atlantic (as some rumours had it) or even try to was moonshine. Similarly the capabilities of western communist parties were much inflated by the bogey element. Even in France, where the prewar communist base had been strengthened by the genuine exploits and inflated propagandist claims of the communist resistance to the Germans, the communist party had to chance of winning power either through elections or otherwise. And had it been otherwise any communist party in western Europe would have been thwarted by the army.

These miscalculations were reflected on the Soviet side where policies were made by Stalin, an elderly prewar figure much battered by the war, innately suspicious and blinkered, moved less by the superficial camaraderie of wartime alliance than by ever-present fears of a new western alliance (including perhaps Germany) against the Soviet Union. Stalin was entirely correct in his assessment of western animosity but entirely incorrect in supposing that his recent allies intended to attack the Soviet Union or were capable of devising means to loose its hold on its European satellites. The principal features of the Cold War were two. The first was its pseudo-ideological trappings. These made it not merely territorial but potentially worldwide. They ensured that in spite of the early victory in the crisis over Berlin in 1949 (which both drew the lines in Europe and ruled out military battles), the Cold War went on and was nourished by the communist victory in China, the Korean War, the successive wars in Vietnam and a chain of open or covert encounters in much of the rest of the world. A by-product of this dramatic expansion of what was initially a tussle for power in Europe, was the amazingly and, for some, disconcertingly swift rehabilitation of Germany and Japan by their western occupiers – with this difference, however: that Germany was to become integrated in international associations (NATO and the European Community) while Japan was to become an independent Power of the first magnitude, much less interested in international politics than in the international economy.

The second main characteristic of the Cold War was the invention of nuclear weapons – weapons rightly regarded as different in kind and not merely the latest stage in the catalogue from the longbow to the tank. These weapons were immensely terrifying but in terms of warmaking almost useless. It took a generation for such a paradox to sink in. The earliest nuclear weapons were weapons of indiscriminate mass destruction and for a brief time only the United States had them. During that period the United States could have used them against the Soviet Union, but although it had used them against Japan and later seriously contemplated using them against China, their use against so recent an ally as the Soviet Union and in time of peace was an impossibility and in any case there was not much left to bomb in the Soviet Union in those first postwar years. And once the Soviet Union acquired a nuclear armoury, however inferior to the American, the suicidal risks of launching a nuclear strike were for both sides prohibitive. An attempt to escape this constraint by inventing more accurate weapons with more limited fields of destruction – medium-range weapons and then tactical or battlefield weapons – was strategically and logically inept. No field commander likes weapons which contaminate the zone into which he proposes to advance and which are more likely to bring anarchy than victory, anarchy being the one thing that scares leaders as much as defeat; and since the deterrent effect of a lesser nuclear weapon depends on the implicit threat to use the next larger one in the chain, the threat to use the less depends on the threat ultimately to use the larger which *ex hypothesi* is ruled out. The development of a chain of nuclear weapons did not eliminate the element of bluff which, although present in all international manoeuvring, was in the case of nuclear weapons too large for their credibility. In so far as nuclear weapons were deterrent, they were mutually deterrent and so politically ineffective. A deterrent is politically effective only when it tips a balance. Nuclear weapons preserved the *status quo* even when the one protagonist was appreciably weaker than the other: that is to say, it preserved imbalance.

Nuclear weapons are so terrible that it is difficult to think sensibly about them. Their chief characteristic is their capacity to kill huge numbers of people, but killing people is not an end in itself (except in the special case of genocide). Killing people is a means to a political end, to changing the mind and policies and actions of any adversary. The use of nuclear weapons in war is a singularly poor means to this end: indiscriminate, and hazardous to the point of suicide. The possession of nuclear arms as a deterrent is an equally poor weapon because it deters an adversary only from doing what it is not in his interest to do. These considerations do not make nuclear weapons insignificant, still less harmless, but they do point to the conclusion that they belong more usefully to the armouries of fanatics than normal powers. The crime of the major Powers has been not in amassing nuclear armouries for themselves – which is folly, not crime – but in doing too little about the spread of nuclear weapons to others.

Thanks to nuclear weapons the Cold War was made to seem a contest between two nearly equal Powers. This was never the case. The United States was at all times more powerful than the Soviet Union not only in the tally of its weaponry but also in the resources which enable it continuously to develop and multiply its weapons and bear the costs of doing so. The costliness of producing and maintaining nuclear weapons on an international scale widened the gap between the two Superpowers until the Soviet Union, incompetently and corruptly governed as well as inherently weaker, was forced to abandon the contest. The inequality of the Superpowers was most clearly attested by the fact that the Soviet Union was destroyed by the Cold War whereas there was never any question of the United States suffering a similar fate. Under Stalin and his successors before Gorbachev, the Soviet Union was trying ever more strenuously to modernise while retaining all the handicaps and vices of an *ancien régime*. This was impossible. The question was not whether the United States could prevail but whether it could do so without suffering unacceptable damage in the process.

The effects of the Cold War on its protagonists were very different. On the Soviet Union they were dramatic and blatant. The Soviet empire in Europe evaporated. The Soviet

Union broke into pieces – seven states in Europe, five in Asia and three in between. The largest of these new states, Russia, was itself threatened with disruption not only through economic collapse but also from some of the twenty ethnic zones which had been allowed a degree of autonomy in the Russian Soviet Republic. Russia's status in the world became profoundly uncertain and its external policies no less so. For the United States the immediate effect of the end of the Cold War was the disappearance of its adversary. The United States was victorious and seemingly supreme. But it was left without the simplistic framework which the Cold War provided for the formation of foreign policies and it had been gravely damaged economically by the Cold War. Its future policies too were uncertain. Politically, the perplexities were most serious in the Middle East (where, as elsewhere, the United States had no settled rationale for its policies beyond antagonism to the Soviet Union); economically, there were perplexities in the determination of a world economic order in which Japan and the European Community were at once sharp competitors but necessary associates.

. . .

II

World War II transformed the Middle East for a second time in thirty years. World War I removed Ottoman Turkish rule over Arabs but the principal beneficiaries were not the Arabs but the British and French who, under international mandates, were given special rights, an approved presence and the right to use armed force to govern the more fruitful parts of the region. During World War II the French were evicted, mainly by the British who also thwarted Italian and German designs to move in. After that war the British tried unsuccessfully to construct a new ersatz-dominion through revived and looser special relationships with Iraq and Egypt, but these countries had had enough of tutelage and the British position was further eroded by the surrender of the mandate over Palestine and the loss in Iran of its oil monopoly, undermined by nationalism and the United States. This transformation from puissant overlord to knowledgeable has-been was rubbed in by the Suez War when Britain, in concert with France and Israel, tried with frenetic folly to overthrow the government of Egypt by force and was stopped by President Eisenhower (even though he too strongly disapproved of Nasser). Besides extinguishing European rule in the Middle East, World War II turned it into an important theatre of the Cold War, lodged in its western flank the state of Israel and, coincidentally, enhanced its international importance: oil, first tapped and despatched westward at the beginning of the century, became much more abundant there through new exploration and discoveries during and after World War II. How to secure supplies for oil-hungry industrial countries added conflict between producers and purchasers to the conflicts of the Cold War. Nor were these the only conflicts, for the Middle East presented also a phenomenon unique in the modern world. It was peopled by men and women who not only professed a particular religion but also believed it with an intensity and near unanimity which no other major religion was able to instil. Conflicts, therefore, could easily become passionate and were commonly expressed in the intractable terms of good and evil since the nationalism animating the region was religious as well as linguistic and territorial.

The Cold War was commonly dubbed ideological, which it never truly was, for there was nothing ideological about the postwar Soviet leadership. Few of these leaders at any level knew or cared about communism or Karl Marx, however often they spouted communist tags. They constituted a clique, or set of interlocking cliques, incompetent and corrupt, whose overriding concern was to monopolise power and keep perks. Their main contribution to dogma was to turn anti-communism into an ideology and so obfuscate the conduct of the Cold War in democratic countries and bring a number of blinkered anti-communists down to the moral and intellectual level of communist bosses. By contrast, collisions between the Middle East and the west were inextricably collisions between Islam and the west – genuinely ideological and characterised by exasperated incomprehension.

Islam makes two fundamental assertions, both of them difficult for non-Muslims to grasp or even credit and difficult for Muslims to reconcile with the modern (often western) trends which many in Islam wish to assimilate more or less. These assertions divide Muslims from non-Muslims and divide Muslims among themselves. The first is the sacred unity of

166

Islam with the consequence, among others, of proscribing or at least looking askance at the existence of separate Muslim states and at the very idea of the state as conceived in the west. Yet states have evolved in the Muslim world as well as beyond it, so that Muslims are troubled to determine whether these states are heretical excrescences or valid entities which are nevertheless subordinate in some ill-defined manner to a larger entity and higher authority. The second and complementary assertion is the overall comprehensive and exclusive authority (under the Koran, properly interpreted) of the Sharia, or Way, which embraces all aspects of communal life as well as personal behaviour and does not recognise the sharp distinction made in the west between the religious and the secular.

For more than a century the Arab world (and Turkey and Iran) had confronted the contradictory needs to fashion a modern economy and society and to preserve or re-assert in a modern context the traditional values and teachings of Islam. The former required learning from the west, the latter required adopting but also rejecting western ways. These concerns were not new. Modernisation had been a prominent theme of debate in the nineteenth century, largely in academic circles in the Arab world since practical politics were largely confined to the Ottoman capital at Istanbul. But by the next century debate was moving to the public arena, the more so as the prospect and then the reality of independence placed upon leaders responsibilities which they had not exercised for centuries. They had to decide what to adopt and what to reject: even the most convinced progressives did not imagine that Comte and Mill could easily be assimilated to Islam and the sheer range of novel ideas was daunting – the place and education of women, the freedom of the individual conscience, regular taxation, equality before the law, organised labour, redistribution of wealth, scientific and technical marvels and much else. They had to decide too how far accepting some of these things might have unpalatable revolutionary consequences and in particular how far a western package of modernising know-how might be inextricably laced with repellent moral laxity. Debate within Islam was therefore also debate about the west, which was for some a storehouse of useful knowledge and ideas, for others (to use Ronald Reagan's phrase about

167

the USSR) the evil empire. To the latter, Saddam Hussein might appear a lesser evil.

In this inflammable climate the United States faced problems not usually found in the province of statecraft and failed to meet them, the incomprehension aggravated by a certain disdain of Arabs. Between the wars British and French power in the Middle East had been constructed around Arabs. The United States, however, tried to construct a strategy around non-Arabs: Israel, Turkey, Iran. While Turkey was courted for its anti-communism rather than its relevance to the Middle East, Iran – traditional adversary of Arabs, not least in the Gulf – became a pillar of the American position until the shah's regime, undermined and overturned by its own excesses, was replaced by a vociferously anti-American successor brandishing its Islamic purity. And the other pillar was Israel, even more abhorrent to Arabs than Iran.

The Nazis' abominable treatment of Europe's Jews had greatly strengthened the urge for a Jewish state and non-Jewish sympathy for it. When the Jews took up arms to get it, Britain renounced the mandate over Palestine which it had exercised since World War I and at the United Nations a plan was adopted for the partition of Palestine into two separate sovereign states, a Palestinian and a Jewish. The Jews purported to accept this plan but negotiated secretly with the Arab emir of Transjordan to nullify it by annexing the proposed Palestinian areas to Transjordan. The refusal to recognise a Palestinian state or identity was and remained a fundamental tenet of Israeli policy. When neighbouring Arab states attacked Israel they suffered a series of defeats; they were unable to destroy the new state which in turn was unable to force them to recognise it. Israel survived with robustness and fervour but could hardly have done so without American support.

This support was on a scale which made it different in kind from American aid to other states. Its sources were many: humane revulsion against the Nazi Holocaust, a thrusting Jewish lobby in the United States, the search for an American bastion in the Middle East. But the cost surpassed expectations as the United States armed Israel with a profusion of sophisticated weapons and underwrote a large part of its domestic budgets as well. With the end of the Cold

War, Israel's strategic value to the United States depreciated but the American enthralment to Israel persisted and prevented the United States from acting as a credible peacemaker in the Middle East or from devising coherent policies for the area.

The postwar Arab world was unique in yet another way. Before the war Iraq was the major source of internationally traded oil in the Middle East. During and after the war oil began to be extracted in great quantities in Kuwait, Saudi Arabia and various Arab principalities in the Gulf. The notion that oil was about to be superseded by nuclear energy proved false and – the biggest change of all – the flow and pricing of the oil came under the control of the states of the region instead of outside corporations and western governments. Thus was posed the question of power, and the use of power, in the Middle East. How were outsiders to secure the oil which they needed, given that the world had turned its back on the simplest method of doing so – by occupying lands which contained it or establishing a quasi-imperial lock over the governments of those lands? Oil was uniquely necessary for industrial countries, their governments had an obligation to make sure that they got it, but the use of force was tabu and even forbidden by the UN Charter which these governments had signed. The Middle East was a region of more than regional importance but there was an uncertainty about how the purchasers of its oil might behave if that oil were denied them. Powerful governments which extolled market forces at home were not happy to rely on them abroad if they were purchasers and what they wanted to purchase was a vital commodity.

Islam is not a world Power and is not about to become one. The very expansion of Islam, eastward to Malaysia and Indonesia, westward to Nigeria and other parts of West Africa, made nonsense of the vision of a single Islamic domain, and a further extension of Islam's sphere of political influence into lately Soviet Central Asia will do more to increase non-Muslim fears of Islamic power than that power itself (conflict between Turkey with its ethnic affinities but no common borders and Iran with readier access but little affinity is only the most obvious source of weakness). Centuries ago the unity of Islam, symbolised by the caliphate, was submerged or even (in some Muslim eyes) extinguished by the triumphs of the Faith in non-Arab lands and by the prevailing of non-Arab peoples who accepted the Faith but obeyed their own ilkhans or sultans rather than a caliph. Yet Arab solidarity is no negligible factor in world affairs. A scheme, which solidified between the wars and is far from dead, envisaged a reconstruction of Syria (modern Syria, Lebanon, Palestine and Jordan) followed by an association between Syria and Iraq, not a unitary state but a permanent partnership not unlike Austria-Hungary after the *Ausgleich* of 1867. Submerging substantial Arab reservations, this scheme would accept the legitimacy of Saudi rule over the Arabian peninsula and seek a looser link between Syria-Iraq and Saudi Arabia, perhaps along the lines of the British Commonwealth after the Statute of Westminster of 1931. Egypt, more Arab than pharaonic since the nineteenth century, would also adhere and so too would a federated Maghreb. The Maghreb Union, like the Gulf Co-operation Council, is a mini-union aspiring to become part of something larger which may never come to be. This version of Arab nationalism, acclimatised to the twentieth century, may be visionary but hardly more so than the European Community before the Treaty of Rome. The Arab world is large and rich, united by a common tongue, and a central component of an Islamic world which is widespread enough and still coherent enough to have a significant impact on international politics and economics, an impact fundamentally different by its nature from any other Power or block of Powers. The shaping of its own affairs is conditioned by the interests and actions of outside Powers, pre-eminently the United States, which cannot afford to let it alone but cannot easily find a *via media* between domination and withdrawal. The first aim of these Powers is stability, in a region easily destabilised by ill-judged intervention. The cultural clash between Islam and the west contains even more potential misunderstanding and miscalculation than those which spurred the Cold War and, given the nature of Islamic beliefs and western material interests, is inextricably political as well as cultural. There is too a nasty touch of contempt on both sides and, being more religious and cultural than economic, it holds a greater propensity for violence than the sharpest economic battles.

. . .

III

Ideas of Islamic unity in or beyond the Middle East contend with the dominant pattern of a world divided into discrete and sovereign states and the multiplication of such states by the application of the principle of self-determination to ever smaller ethnic groups (or groups claiming an ethnic identity). In the Middle East this dominant states pattern is relatively novel and imported, but in western Europe it is so firmly established as to be regarded as a fact of nature. Yet here too it has been queried in the half century after World War II. The main reasons have been, first, the seemingly inevitable and menacing preponderance of Germany in any states system in Europe and, secondly, the decline of western European states in relation to the economic power of the United States and the military power of the Soviet Union. A second European war against an overmighty Germany and the defeat of Germany by a non-European state in a purely adventitious alliance with a barely European state forced radical thoughts into European minds. But fear of Russia did not cancel fear of Germany: there were now two fears and for forty years the problem of handling the one in the context of the other.

In 1945 the relative decline of Europe and the emergence of the Soviet threat were more pressing concerns than a German revival, so that an association of western Europe with the United States took precedence over the reorganisation of western Europe as a union or federation instead of a clutch of competitive sovereign states. When, however, the Cold War and the Soviet menace receded, the political and economic configuration of Europe – the question whether or not to put the states system into reverse – took first place. It did so in a context changed by the dissolution of Soviet power. Whereas plans for a European union had taken shape in a divided Europe, the fledgling European Community of (mainly) western states was obliged from the late 1980s to review its course in the context of Europe as a reintegrated whole: the end of the Cold War restored the concept of Europe as a meaningful political term. But although the demise of the Soviet empire abolished the division of

171

Europe into two parts, it did not expunge the considerable differences – notably economic but also political – between west and east which had existed before the forty-year Soviet overlay of the east. The trend in western Europe towards some kind of union which must involve some erosion of sovereignty was not matched in eastern Europe where, on the contrary, the recovery of independence at the end of the 1980s hallowed the idea of sovereignty and prompted also the creation of new sovereignties by breaking up the old. The experience of the interwar years and of World War II itself had shaken faith in the west in the adequacy of the state, but in the east Soviet domination and homogenisation had the opposite effect.

For western Europe there was a further complication, for when Europe ceased to be sandwiched between two Superpowers the western sector became uncertain about its relationship with the United States, military protector but also trade rival. The need for American troops became hard to perceive – and hard to justify to American taxpayers – while the general economic climate exacerbated commercial conflict between the European Community and the United States. When in the late 1940s the United States had resolved to remain present and powerful in Europe in order to contain Soviet power, western Europeans welcomed this resolve and the NATO alliance gave it form and substance. Plans for a European union, first formalised in the Treaty of Rome in 1957, were overshadowed by the anti-Soviet concerns of the North Atlantic Treaty of 1949. Fifty years later the priorities were reversed by the most momentous events in Europe since the signing of the NATO treaty: the end of the Cold War and the consequent reunification of Germany.

The first seeds of the European Community were sown before World War II ended by Europeans who were worried about a recurrent German problem. After the defeat of Germany in World War I, the victors looked for ways of keeping Germany weak. In the event Germany recovered its strength and started another European war within twenty years of losing the first. The lesson was not lost on Germany's near neighbours (Belgium, the Netherlands) who realised that attempts to keep Germany down were futile and that in any case they themselves needed a prosperous Germany to buy their products. These reflections led to the conclusion that the states system no longer served the purposes which it had served for three centuries – roughly from the end of the Thirty Years War. A European community or union was conceived as an antidote to German power, whose weight in the middle of Europe was a standing threat to peace and stability. Such a community or union would encapsulate Germany, create a field for German ambitions within rather than against Europe, and would also maximise its members' joint economic enterprise and even perhaps create an economic power in the same category as the United States and Japan. When these ideas were embraced by both France and Germany they became a political reality.

They contributed to the transformation of Germany where the western sectors, revivified by American money and their own skills and discipline, became a success story in alliance with many of their former victors and victims. German economic success was crucial to the development of a European union. If, as Adam Smith observed, there were few ways in which a man can be more innocently employed than in making money (a one-sided but by no means erroneous judgement), it was crucial for the Federal Republic to be more successful than the Weimar Republic had been in 1919–33. The Weimar Republic gave way to the Third Reich largely because it was buffeted by economic storms at its inception and again at its end. The Federal Republic by contrast was a conspicuous success for decades but the reunification of Germany upon the collapse of communist rule in the east posed economic problems greater than any experienced by the Federal Republic since its creation; and these problems were the more serious for Germany's neighbours because by this date West Germany's very success had made it the linchpin of the European Community.

Bonn's response to the challenges of reunification were more political than economic. The costs were subordinated to the greatness of the occasion and the terms set for the integration of the two currencies were designed to win the hearts and minds of east Germans for the ruling party in West Germany. Bonn offered to exchange east German for west German marks at parity. It also seriously underestimated the costs of regenerating the east German economy and resolved to meet these costs by borrowing rather than taxation. These decisions entailed risks of inflation which were countered by high interest rates which, given the dominance of the German currency throughout the European Community, obliged Germany's neighbours and partners to raise their own interest rates or at least not lower them, thus smothering hopes of economic growth in the whole Community as a consequence of the rescue and refinancing of east Germany. Since one of the Community's prime purposes was mutual economic prosperity, these measures soured the communal mood, disjointed communal financial institutions and obstructed plans to turn the community into a closer unit sooner rather than later.

The Community possessed many of the principal ingredients of power. It had material resources, industrial and technological skills, good education, good government and political stability. But it lacked the essential engine of institutions capable of taking decisions and implementing them; and it lacked the will, or enough will, to remedy this defect. A number of its members, among whom Britain was the most obstructive, wanted the material benefits of association without the abandonment of national sovereignty (often rhetorically confused with national identity). Others believed that the Community's aims could not be attained without steady and reasonably fast progress from commercial to financial, economic and political union. The central political and constitutional issue, which was over the division of powers between levels of government, focused opposition in which legitimate fears were powerfully reinforced by emotional prejudices. After protracted discussion during the 1970s and 1980s the Treaty of Maastricht was signed in 1991 to supplement the Treaty of Rome which was by this date thirty-four years old. The Treaty of Maastricht was signed by all twelve members of the Community. It created a European Union; a single citizenship of this Union in addition to separate national citizenship; and a European Council of heads of government with the president of the Commission; and it envisaged the gradual development of joint foreign and defence policies and joint action on a number of other common problems such as drug trafficking, immigration, terrorism and other serious crimes. Within the Union the Community was to pursue economic integration and the treaty set conditions and a timetable for the introduction of a single currency and a central bank by the end of the century.

174

Constitutionally the treaty did next to nothing to modify the dominant position of the Council of Ministers or to enhance that of the parliament. The Council of Ministers, composed of heads of state or government each armed with a veto over the more important decisions (the organ which decided whereas the Commission in Brussels might only recommend or implement), remained the ultimate authority, but the treaty was a symbol of the resolve to develop the Community into a Union with power gradually seeping away from state governments and parliaments.

The treaty's economic purposes were buffeted by recession and the travails of German unification. Its political aims were skewered in embryo by the wars in Yugoslavia which embarrassingly displayed the inability of the Community to make up its collective mind about what ought to be done or how to do it. Critics of the Community ridiculed its incompetence while supporters proclaimed the need for closer and stronger central institutions. The Community was at this stage as ill-equipped to formulate or implement common external policies as it was ill-prepared to complete its economic and monetary union. Yet few supposed that it would atrophy or melt away. On the contrary, some twenty states were seeking to join it, in some form at some time. If, however, a large number of them were admitted they would turn the Community into an organisation like the Organisation of American States or the Organisation of African Unity, an association of sovereign states much less coherent and much less effective than the body envisaged by the Treaty of Rome. One threat to the Community was its popularity which threatened, by expanding it, to turn it into a sideshow.

The prospects for the European Union depend on its resourcefulness in reconciling its very existence with the continuing vigour of nationalism and the state. Conceived with political and economic purposes which, albeit in entirely different ways, marked a reaction against a states system, the Union jolted Europe's two most self-consciously nationalist states, France and Britain. The British accepted the Community as a regrettable economic necessity but did not like it or much bother to think about it; English politicians either evaded the debate or cast it in emotional superficialities one way or the other. France, by contrast, determined to adopt the Community and play a central role in it with Germany.

While France thus aimed to get the best of two worlds, Britain fell into the trap of getting the worst without arresting the Community's development or turning it into channels less distasteful to the British. What made French policy more sensible than British was the peculiar state of western Europe at the end of World War II. Besides the factors undermining the states system were the exceptional congruence and compatibility of the states themselves. Until the second defeat of Germany there was a fundamental incompatibility between France, Britain and their neighbouring democracies on the one hand and the undemocratic structures and mentalities of, in particular, Germany; but the wars fought to curb German power had also the effect of changing the nature of the German state and, to put it crudely but not inaccurately, making Germany part of western Europe. In this transformed situation, which still exists and seems likely to persist, the European Union as something beyond an adventitious alliance became possible and robust. The Cold War overshadowed it; the ending of the Cold War caught it coincidentally at an awkward moment in its development; but it survives as a significant, if still inchoate, force not only in Europe but in the world.

. . .

IV

At the approach of a new century there were in the world at large two universal actors: the United States and the United Nations, the one with power and the other without. There was therefore a question of how far and on what terms the one would lend power to the other, and for what purposes.

The United States was, absolutely as well as relatively, uniquely powerful in the possession of modern armed forces larger than those of any other state or possible coalition of states, and in the capacity to deploy these forces anywhere in the world. The disappearance of the Soviet Union demonstrated this extraordinary predominance, unprecedented in history, but there was also a cost which was not so quickly appreciated. The concentration of money and research on the Cold War had diverted material and human resources to a hazardous extent, sacrificing the domestic economy, the external balance of payments, the health, wealth and stability of American society, and calling in question the cherished, at one time axiomatic, position of the United States as the world's leading economic power – a blow to national pride and confidence and a temptation to protectionism and demagogic rhetoric.

The principal outward and visible sign of this shift in power between the beginning and the end of the Cold War was the frightening accumulation of debt: the national debt, personal and corporate debt, budgetary deficits and external deficits (the last extending to invisibles as well as trade in commodities). Such burdens could be borne only by steady and substantial economic growth but in the closing decades of the century the rate of growth was declining.

The strength and prestige of the United States in the twentieth century were grounded in its industrial inventiveness and efficiency, the volume of its output and the paving of its own streets with gold: it had been a by-word for economic success since the beginning of the century and after World War II it was in a class of its own. It had, also if less securely, a reputation for tempering the rough edges of capitalist economies with liberal values (democratic values, social programmes and the denunciation of colour prejudice). It inspired hopes, not fears or distaste. Americans themselves and others expected the United States to combine with ease endless material and social progress at home with the leading role in international affairs, economic and political – to spend huge sums of money and be able to afford to do so. The Cold War necessitated massive government expenditure and the end of the Cold War seemed initially to make such expenditure more fruitful by removing from the tally its most burdensome and least productive item. The sacrifices had been worthwhile, for even if the Reagan administration had not deliberately driven its adversary into dissolution by raising the economic stakes, that was what had happened; and without the Cold War the money could be used for more amiable and more productive purposes, and books could be made to balance. If the United States had won because it was richer, the riches must be there and could be put to better use than making war.

On second thoughts, however, there was room for the suspicion that the United States had overcome, if not the wrong enemy, at least not the chief one. The Soviet Union had turned out to be something like a paper tiger, a foe not altogether worthy of American steel, while the Cold War had promoted the rehabilitation and rise of Japan with a more enduring challenge to American supremacy. As with Germany, so with Japan the haste to forgive and forget World War II in order to prosecute the Cold War enabled the Japanese economy to prosper hugely. Its economic progress, analogous to that of the United States during World War II, enabled it to bid fair to become the centre of a vast economic zone extending over eastern, south-eastern and southern Asia and even Australasia.

For a quarter of a century after World War II the regulator of the world's economic affairs was the Bretton Woods system formalised on lines dictated by the United States to enshrine free trade and secure stable international exchange rates. The system was nourished by the dollar which, alone among currencies, was defined in relation to gold and was intended to serve as an international as well as a national medium of exchange. But the system broke down, destroyed by a superfluity of dollars dispensed by the United States to pay for its foreign strategic commitments on top of its imports. This profusion destroyed the value of the dollar and forced the United States to suspend the convertibility of the dollar into gold and allow it to be devalued by about one-third. The vertiginous rises in the price of oil in the same decade – the 1970s – further ravaged the system. Exchange rates were left to float and international regulation became a battle between, on the one side, short-term expedients devised by governments and central banks (often by telephone) and, on the other, speculators with an interest in destabilising the markets in which they were fishing. Modern communications technology helped the latter more than the former and so aggravated the instability. This failure in economic management damaged the standing of the United States in particular since it had been deemed to be the one Power sufficiently puissant and intelligent to run a world economic order. The dollar, like the German mark in the smaller sphere of Europe, turned out to be a strikingly strong currency without being strong enough to do all the things required of it – whether the Soviet Union existed or not.

The attempt to do too much was a failure in statesmanship. It was a failure in circumstances of incomparable difficulty but it was needlessly exacerbated by stupid profligacy in the 1980s when the presidencies of Reagan and Bush turned the United States into the world's biggest debtor and robbed it of much of the esteem in which it had been held. If, after the Cold War, the principal duel was to be with Japan (and perhaps with the European Community too) the drift of American policy would be towards regionalism and protectionism – the reverse of the aspirations of Bretton Woods and a potentially calamitous reversion to beggar-my-neighbour economics. The United States began to develop an American economic zone comprising, besides itself, Canada and Mexico in a free trade area (NAFTA), but it did so half-heartedly and against fears that American industry would move into Mexico while Mexicans flooded into the United States. In the vague future, parts of South America might be added to this zone but not without reservations about its political predictability and the possibility of its gravitating instead to a Japanese-Pacific zone. All such zones have a certain illusoriness; they look more compact and coherent on the map than they do on a more rigorous analysis which reveals discrepancies within them which may overstrain the economies or the goodwill of the stronger partners. From this aspect the strains in the existing European Community – between, for example, the extremes of Germany and Greece – seem less damaging than those likely to arise in an American zone or a Japanese. NAFTA particularly lacks the logic which could make it a harmonious counterweight to the European Community; it could do more to weaken than strengthen the economic weight of the United States in the world.

Japan, whose national product in 1950 had been a tenth of that of the United States, had become a hugely successful manufacturing and exporting country without appearing unduly bothered by the conflict between globalism and regionalism: it meant to have the best of both. Its attributes of determination, good training, rigorous regimentation and technical ingenuity were bolstered by exceptionally low military spending and, in the 1970s, by a capacity to take at critical moments bold decisions which turned out to be right: for example and momentously, the invention of a new deal on Middle East oil – new on pricing and on delivery terms – which undercut western purchasers and catapulted the price of oil without wrecking the Japanese economy; and simultaneously and at bold cost, replacing a successful economic base by a new one in automation and robotics. Twenty years later there lurked doubts whether its tightly drilled educational and industrial regimes might be the best base from which to face the increasingly rapid tempo of technological change; and whether Japan, learning from its own traditions and the American example, had nevertheless not overlooked one major element in the German postwar experience: the value of cooperation between capital and labour, government and unions (the element which, in Britain, Thatcherism, putting political prejudice before economic sense, had spurned). Japan was a global economic macropower and also undisputed king in a zone which embraced the bustling economies of Korea, Taiwan and Singapore and a host of lesser fry round the Pacific ring and in South East Asia. Although the confrontation between Japan and the United States lacked the brio of the clash of arms, it was not without bitterness, incomprehension once again, and extravagant bombast – as, for example, when President Bush proclaimed that the United States must place the American flag on Mars in order to sharpen the edge of American competitiveness and Japan proclaimed its intention to plant a colony on that planet in the year 2057.

Japan's miraculous economic rise bemused onlookers. That rise has shown signs of halting but competitors' hopes of a severe or permanent check are probably misplaced. Japan may face fresh choices as hazardous as those which it successfully confronted in the 1970s and it may find that these new choices cannot so easily be made, as were the earlier ones, in comparative isolation from the rest of the world: it will need to temper competitiveness with a larger dash of cooperation. Its prime competitor will still be the United States but given the existence of other comparable economic entities it will to some extent be free to play *fortiter* in one direction and *suaviter* in another.

It has been common to speak of three major economic conglomerates – a flexible rather than a starkly bipolar pattern – but the identity of the third player is perhaps changing. In the European Union national centrifugalism is blocking the realisation of its economic potential so that it risks missing the economic tide, while on the other hand China has come into view as a possible Third Force – the world's third most copious producer of goods and services (after the United States and Japan), registering record rates of economic growth, recovering Hong Kong at the end of the century and not despairing of a special and specially rewarding relationship with Taiwan; but trying to spread its economic wings in a tightly pinioned political system, a hazardous equivocation. Both China and Russia, and India too, are teaching for a market system on the western capitalist model without realising that in modern capitalism one of the most potent forces in the market place is that of the speculators – a malign force which can turn a free market into an open field for rogues smarter than politicians. Africa is in limbo, marginalised by the end of the Cold War, no longer of much interest to the United States (which had no policies for Africa beyond anti-communism), and oppressed by fragmentation, bad government, famines and disease, a population explosion, unmanageable debt and the loss of the spirited hopes of independence. These ills have been more than enough to destroy the unexpressed but underlying assumption at independence that new states could be modernised and put on their feet in a decade or two. With the end of the Cold War Africa fell out of international politics. It shows few signs of playing any significant role in international economics and holds a leading role only in the call for aid. Economic improvement depends on foreign funds, chiefly from the World Bank and the International Monetary Fund which insist on concomitant economic measures which, since they inflict hardship on the bulk of the people, can be carried through only by dictators. The remaining great land mass – Antarctica – can, for all its reputed wealth, be left for some time to the likes (if there be any) of Sir Ranulf Fiennes.

. . .

V

The United Nations is an international body with a contradiction at its core. It is an association of sovereign states which has been brought into existence by those states in order to curb or remedy the shortcomings of the state. It affirms the sovereignty of the state and proscribes – except in special circumstances – any international intervention in matters which are 'essentially within the domestic jurisdiction' of the state, but its effectiveness in relation to its prime purpose may require such intervention. The United Nations is a global essay in moderating the interplay between independence and interdependence in a world where interdependence is inescapable but often unpalatable. Independence and interdependence are no longer alternatives. They are part of an essential symbiosis. The world has become one in some aspects but not in others and it does not feel like one.

The state is an outstanding fact. It has identity, territorial definition, legitimacy, the capacity to take decisions and to organise and deploy power; it commands loyalty and is widely, if mistakenly, regarded as a natural phenomenon. People dissatisfied with the state in which they live commonly wish to live in or form another. Yet the state may also be inadequate or even dangerous. Its prosperity depends on other states; the quality of life within it is often debased by negligent or tyrannical governments; and it makes war.

The immunity of the state from regulation or restraint has never gone unchallenged, notably from the laws of war circumscribing the state's right to go to war and its behaviour in the conduct of war. Sovereignty has never been untrammelled. Moralists, lawyers and statesmen have conceded the existence of something above or beyond the state which restrains the state and its governors.

The United Nations, like the League of Nations, was created in the hope of reducing the number of wars between states. The League had been judged a failure in as much as it had not prevented or curbed wars in various parts of the world during the 1920s and 1930s, but these failures were interpreted as a need for a better League, not for none. The United Nations, therefore, was the League relaunched with, in particular, wider powers and a wider membership. But, departing from the pattern of the League, the UN had also a wider purpose than keeping international peace. In terms not to be found in the Covenant of the League, the UN Charter expounded the duty of the United Nations to promote certain principles and standards of behaviour (e.g. equal rights, non-discrimination, respect for human rights).

To fulfil these commitments, the UN would be bound sometimes to intervene in the domestic affairs of a state. Yet article 2 (7) of the Charter ruled out such intervention except in the context of a threat to or breach of the peace or an act of aggression – all of which preconditions were assumed to mean international peace or international aggression, not disorders within a state with no impact on relations between states. Article 2 (7) established a basic rule immunising the state from international intervention unless the Security Council resolved that international peace had been broken or endangered. If, however, the Security Council did so find, then the provisions of Chapter VII of the Charter came into operation and article 2 (7) no longer applied.

Intervention can take many forms from diplomatic pressures through economic and other non-military measures to the use of armed force and Chapter VII draws a line between non-forcible measures and the use of force. The former may be imposed by the Security Council and all members are obliged to implement them. The latter may also be imposed by the Council but any member may choose not to participate in them. The distinction is between the measures to be adopted and not between the aims to be achieved. Once the Council has passed a resolution which brings Chapter VII into operation – that is to say, has resolved that a certain state of affairs exists – any of the measures foreseen in Chapter VII may be applied. The exclusion of article 2 (7) hinges, therefore, on a finding of fact by the Council.

In practice members of the Council, and none more so than the five permanent members with the right of veto, have been reluctant to resort to Chapter VII. The Council has acted on dozens of occasions under Chapter VI but rarely under Chapter VII. Chapter VI, on the peaceful settlement of disputes, allows the Council to investigate the causes of disputes and recommend procedures for settling them, again in the context of a threat to international peace and security; and under this chapter the United Nations has despatched a series of missions to monitor cease-fire agreements, patrol armistice lines, observe and report on elections. Such missions, neither large nor costly (their total annual cost in the 1990s was no more than 1 per cent of the US military budget), are designed to keep the peace but not to make peace or intervene in a war; and they may not enter upon the territory of a member state without that state's consent. They have been increasingly in demand all over the world but they are inappropriate in the graver conflicts envisaged by Chapter VII, and one of the main weaknesses of the United Nations, like the League, has been its impotence in the face of these graver conflicts which are, by definition, the acknowledged threats to world peace. Chief among the sources of this weakness are the aversion of member states to erode the principle of state sovereignty; the paucity of the UN's information and diplomatic services and its lack, therefore, of timely warnings of trouble to come; and the lack of forces of its own to inject promptly into a critical situation. The United Nations has been further handicapped by the recurrent refusal of its principal members to pay their agreed shares of the expenses, both regular budgetary expenses and the costs of special missions.

A standard explanation for the UN's disappointing performance in peacekeeping has been the incidence of the Cold War. Most modern wars are short but the Cold War lasted for some forty years during which it turned the United Nations into an area of Superpower conflict and suffocated the mechanisms designed to keep the peace and ameliorate the human condition. Yet to ascribe to the Cold War all the blame for the atrophy of the UN is an insecure judgement since it assumes that the UN would have performed very differently in the absence of the Cold War. But the United Nations does only what its members will it to do and in the euphoria of victory in 1945 the Charter – notably in the renunciation by members of the right to make war except in self-defence and the transfer to the Security Council of the right to use armed force – moved well ahead of what governments, perhaps people too, thought proper for an international body: many of these governments came to think that they had gone too far. The Cold War was a convenient excuse for refusing to enable the UN to do what its founders had hoped it might do. The end of the Cold War did not extinguish these reservations.

There was, however, a second development, contemporary with the Cold War but more enduring. This was an unforeseen change in the principal sources of death and devastation. At the end of World War II violent death connoted above all death in wars between states, the kind of aggression which the Kellog-Briand Pact as well as the Covenant and the Charter had hoped to make less frequent, but over the next fifty years there was no war of that sort while there was a terrible toll of misery and horror from civil war and domestic tyranny. In one country alone – Sudan – at least one million people died in civil wars, and the barbarous regimes of Idi Amin, Bokassa, Pol Pot and others in other countries did their hideous work without posing any certifiable threat to international peace. From these horrors, morally intolerable and also within the express compass of the UN's duties, there grew a wish to draw a new distinction between international intervention to prevent state wars and international intervention for humanitarian purposes – a highly contentious venture if, for example, the humanitarian purposes could not be achieved without overthrowing the government, perhaps democratically elected, of a member state. The Charter's repeated emphasis on the observance of human rights and on an international duty to see them observed (in, for example, articles 1 (3) and 55) appear to legitimise and even require such intervention and in 1991 the Security Council resolved to sanction the use of armed force to protect the Kurds of northern Iraq without invoking Chapter VII and in defiance of the legitimate government of Iraq. It did so for mainly emotional reasons: revulsion against the persecution of these Kurds and President Bush's obsession with Saddam Hussein (not unlike Anthony Eden's feelings about Nasser in 1956). Legally, however, this kind of intervention, besides being unavailable to Kurds in Turkey or elsewhere, did not square easily with the letter of the Charter unless the phrase in article 2 (7) 'essentially within the domestic jurisdiction of any state' were to be interpreted to mean that, beyond a certain limit, outrageous behaviour ceased to count as domestic because it stirred international indignation and fears or, more pertinently, infringed international Conventions signed by the state accused of the misdeeds. The resolve to help the Kurds of Iraq was a departure hoping to become a precedent, but without a series of similar interventions it would remain eccentric, not securely a part of the law of the Charter. A case for humanitarian intervention arises when the humanitarian purpose is paramount, but it is rash to suppose that the humanitarian purpose may be easily or entirely divorced from other and less humanitarian purposes.

The prospects for law and order in the world in the coming century lie first and foremost and overwhelmingly with the United States – a daunting outlook for Americans and not a comfortable one for others. American power and American action are indispensable. But they are not enough since American power, although it can reach all corners of the world, is not so great that it can be deployed in many places at once nor is it sufficiently underpinned by the American economy to do so for any length of time. The United States is not in a condition to be a universal policeman.

That the United Nations is not a universal policeman needs no argument nor was it designed to be one. It was created by major Powers in order to provide rules and mechanisms for international action in many fields, particularly in keeping the peace and extending the rule of law between and, more tentatively, within states. It cannot act in a given situation without the assent and active cooperation of major Powers, among which the United States is pre-eminent.

The United States has a choice. That is one of the advantages of being a major Power and also one of the responsibilities. The United States may choose to act on its own after the fashion of an imperial Power or it may choose to lead the United Nations. A state which has power, clear-cut interests and a belief in the rightness of its aims and judgements has self-evidently practical reasons for acting on its own. Moreover, imperial action is easier than it once was since modern technologies enable power to be brought to bear without the conquest and occupation of foreign territory, formerly the hallmarks of imperialism – but lustily decried by the United States. Yet the arguments against proceeding in this way remain overwhelming, morally objectionable, entangling and expensive (the Gulf War, initiated and led by the United States, was underwritten by others). Further, imperialism by whatever means now for the first time in history has to be geographically limited. The British at the height of their extraordinary world power famously chose not to try to add China to their empire, but if the United States wishes to fashion a world in which its own interests will be safeguarded and its values promoted it has to be willing and able to act throughout the world. That it cannot do by itself. The alternative is action through and in concert with the United Nations. The temptation is to try to do a bit of both at once. Trying to get the best of two worlds is not intrinsically bad but trying and failing may be calamitous: in Somalia the United Sates played an inconsistent double game at some cost to itself and at much cost to the United Nations and the UN's purposes, while in Haiti it mounted under UN colours an American operation declared by the president to be neither a peacekeeping operation nor one designed to prevent atrocities or abuses of human rights.

The Gulf War of 1991 was a warning. In that emergency the United States aimed to eject the Iraqis from Kuwait, to safeguard the flow of oil and to overthrow Saddam Hussein. The means were American armed forces and an international alliance under the aegis of the United Nations. The alliance was formed to liberate Kuwait by whatever means might be necessary, including force, but the aims of the alliance did not extend to the overthrow of Saddam Hussein, to which some of the allies were opposed. There was, therefore, some duplicity on the American side. There was also confusion and a loss of nerve when the Iraqi government did not collapse and no successful conspiracy against Saddam Hussein materialised: Bush did not so much plan Saddam's downfall as hope for it and then leave it to others. The successful liberation of Kuwait, achieved through American action in concerting UN action, was overshadowed by the onslaught on Iraq which was indiscriminately devastating and a failure. The attempt to change the government of Iraq under cover of, but without the clear sanction of, the United Nations was inept and shortsighted in as much as it diminished the credit of the United States at the UN and skewered American policy-making for the future in the Middle East. The United States demonstrated its power, which was not in dispute, and its resolve, which was; but these demonstrations aside, the United States, by trying to straddle two worlds, got the worst of both. It failed to secure its national aims and failed to fortify its international leadership. It also failed to pay for its wars which were financed by thrusting the begging bowl under Japanese and sundry Arab noses.

The aftermath of the Gulf War raised a further question. What was begun as a riposte to a blatantly aggressive breach of international peace and security turned into a muddle about international responsibility for protecting internal minorities against domestic repression. If, with the Cold War over, more use was to be made of the United Nations, what was the UN to be used for? To deal with dangers or, also, with horrors? Not all horrors are international dangers. The horrors in Somalia were dangerous to nobody outside Somalia. It was not obvious that the horrors in Bosnia threatened international peace (although probably they did). Yet the clamour for the United Nations to intervene, to do something, is more insistent in the face of horrors than in the face of threats to peace and breaches of international law, and it would incontestably be a great service if the UN were able to mitigate the former. If, for whatever reason, it cannot do so it is folly to raise false expectations which, upon being disappointed, impair the UN's standing and its capacity to confront its more surely established duties.

The Cold War put a premium on what came to be called crisis management and on impromptu action for the short term. Crises will continue to occur and require to be managed, but with the end of the Cold War it is opportune to insist that the exigencies of crisis, while they may concentrate attention and effort, tend also to put aside the essential questions of what the United Nations is entitled to do and what it is equipped to do. And these questions cannot be reviewed simply in the light of what was intended in 1945 because the course of events during the Cold War and in the few years since it ended has shown up the ambiguities in the Charter's scheme for keeping the peace as well as the pathetic uselessness of many of the attempts to cope with crises.

A crisis demands prompt action which is often dubiously legitimate, dubiously effective and alarmingly dependent on an impossible degree of luck. Crises generate confusion which damages the United Nations itself without always succouring its intended beneficiaries. The Iraqi Kurds, for instance, were protected for a while by the safe havens created for them by some of the victors of the Gulf War but their plight in Saddam Hussein's Iraq – neglected by the outside world for years and then worsened by Bush's attempt to use them to topple Saddam – was at best temporarily relieved by the safe havens and bound to sink once more into oblivion as the war receded into the past and, with it, the international commitment to the Kurds and international funds for their salvation. The UN's right to intervene in

Iraq otherwise than to liberate Kuwait was uncertain; and if Saddam's treatment of the Kurds and Shi'ites warranted intervention it was still uncertain whether the Charter gave the Security Council authority to protect them in Saddam's Iraq or extended to the demolition of Saddam's regime as the only means to make them safe.

Bosnia provided an even more confusing conundrum. However the events leading to war in that republic might be interpreted, the essential fact was the determination of Serbia and Croatia to partition and annex all or most of it. The European Union, with unimpeachable intentions, American encouragement and almost unexampled unpreparedness, assumed the functions and responsibilities of a regional organisation for Europe, although it was no such thing: its competence was limited to the territories of its member states. The EU was very tentatively exploring mechanisms for concerting common foreign policies but had not got far, had precluded for the time being the development of common defence (i.e. military) policies, had in relation to Yugoslavia no unity of purpose and was additionally hampered by the constitutional incapacity of its keenest champion of intervention (Germany) to send troops beyond its borders. The chief consequence of the EU's pathetic attempts to run before it could walk were to keep the United Nations, the competent body, in the shadows and give the impression of a split between the UN and the EU. The UN, departing from established practice, sent small and scattered protective units to areas where no peace had yet been imposed or negotiated with the result that they became helpless, useless and in some cases hostages.

The tasks in Bosnia were various, to some extent contradictory but also inseparable. They were: protecting, feeding and rescuing civilian victims of the fighting; protecting these protectors; negotiating local or general truces and policing them; securing an end to the fighting and a political settlement by argument or threats of military action. The protection of victims and rescuers required a measure of goodwill from the combatants but a political settlement, whether negotiated or imposed, must earn the ill will of some, if not all, of them. The use of force, otherwise than by humanitarian units in self-defence, was arguably outside the competence of the United Nations, arguably ineffective in one or other

189

of the forms mooted (air strikes, ground operations) and certainly unpalatable to states who might be asked to contribute forces without a time limit. There was more argument and room for argument than action. In Somalia contemporaneously, Bush, with his hopes of re-election fading, embarked on two barely compatible courses. He offered to reinforce the UN's (ineffectual) UNOSOM with 3,000 American troops and prepared at the same time an independent American expedition ten times as big which was to ease the flow of food, medicines etc. He also undertook to leave Somalia at the end of a few months, a commitment which effectually precluded the disarming of the factions which were looting 10–20 per cent of the supplies. And he set in train a course, pursued by Clinton, which, so far from supporting the UN's attempts to pacify and reconcile the warring factions, developed into an attempt to destroy the strongest of them and kill its leader, Aideed (whom at first the United States had favoured against his rivals). Again contemporaneously, John Major was insisting that in Bosnia British forces serving with the UN forces would be exposed to no unacceptable risk, without explaining how you measure the acceptability of risk or why armed forces should be used only in risk-free operations. So long as governments and people believe that their armed forces should risk life and limb in defence of their own state but not of anything else, international action is severely, even farcically, constrained. In Bosnia the United States (and others) fought shy of using force on the ground when a little of it might have done much good, and then after three years of war imposed the Dayton Accord which stopped the fighting at the cost of creating purely ethnic states, an unreal and vicious solution.

. . .

VI

The end of the Cold War was the end of an epoch, an epoch distinguished by its nature rather than by its length. The main characteristics of the end of an epoch is the temptation to make too much of it. The Cold War lasted half a century or a little less. Like the Thirty Years War, for example, it defined its epoch in terms of hostilities, emotions, sometimes actions, but not in terms of those persistent forces called ideas: intellectually it was a barren epoch. It was not an epoch in the sense that, in Europe, the Renaissance or the Age of Discovery or the Enlightenment denote a stir in ideas. The Cold War, by concentrating minds on a transient phenomenon, promoted little that survived it. In the long run it will be seen as having done more to blanket or interrupt than to change the course of events and for this reason its immediate aftermath was curiously disconcerting, as full of worries and perplexity and hesitations as of rejoicing or relief.

When after World War I the Habsburg and Ottoman empires dissolved, they left not a wrack behind. The Tsarist empire, however, did. It was reborn, but only to suffer a most peculiar fate. In time it too suffered the fate of all empires but neither in war nor as the result of war. It succumbed or imploded through economic inadequacy without the added thump of lost military battles, and that is the first of the principal, if still provisional, conclusions to be drawn about the Cold War: that a powerful super-state may be shot to pieces without shots being fired; that economic war between sufficiently embittered adversaries may be as catastrophic as war waged by more conventional means. Perhaps the Cold War was an embryonic prototype of an economic war between the United States and Japan. (It would, however, be foolish to suppose that there will never again be a Russian state in the upper ranks of a global states system.)

Secondly, the collapse of the Soviet empire has provided the most cogent modern illustration of the immemorial interaction of universalism and particularism. As the Soviet empire broke up abroad and at home into its particular components, these parts proclaimed the force of centrifugal self-determination, for whatever the impact of anti-imperialist resentment and anti-governmental indignation, what emerged from the convulsions – from Poland and Estonia to Turkestan and Tadjikistan through Ukraine and Georgia – were old national identities asserting their territorial, religious and linguistic selves against each other as much as against their cast-off rulers. These new–old identities are more relevant to the future than the Soviet empire which had become a thing of the past. Yet elsewhere in the world the opposite was in the ascendant. Much of Europe

– the more prosperous parts – was seeking integration in defiance of self-determination and running up against national identities in the process. Opposition to the Treaty of Maastricht in many member states of the Community, and popular hostility to the Community in countries (Switzerland, for example) whose governments had formally applied to join it, showed how easily leaders may misjudge their followers over issues as profound as the defining of the political habitat. In the American continent too, where the United States was toying with a more restricted form of integration through free trade agreements with Canada and Mexico, second thoughts disclosed comparable confusions and unease about measures which seemed to undermine the familiar certainties of the sovereign state without, however, proposing or even envisaging more comprehensive integration, functional or geographical. A North American commercial zone beyond the state but well short of a union was essentially adversarial as well as regional, a way to bolster the economy of the United States against Japan and the European Union by recourse to a degree of integration not too offensive to particularist emotions and traditions.

Thirdly, the flux and reflux of these forces, veiled by the Cold War but independent of it, are governed by states which alone have the capacity to create organisations of states. These organisations, more constructed than evolved, lack distinctive voices of their own. The imperatives of integration are largely, but not entirely, economic: the bulwarks of particularism are *mentalités*, states of mind. The practical issue is how much of one is worth how much of the other. To such a question there is no mathematical answer. It presents a case for leadership, not demonstration; for judgement and persuasion beyond calculation or gut reaction. What is at issue is beyond meterial well-being and beyond national pride and spirit. It is the preservation and increase of order in the world: first, in the reduction of war by the regulation of conflicts without war (hot or cold, military or economic) and, secondly, order through the active defence and promotion of internal peace and justice, good government and human happiness. These were the aims of statesmen and others in 1945 before the Cold War set in and of many earlier generations, and the Cold War did not change them. They are political aims whose advancement depends on political organisations and mechanisms and the willingness of political figures to use them. Whether the *polis* is a city state or a wider society created by perennially expanding technology (particularly communications technology) affects not the aims themselves but the means appropriate to their pursuit. In this perspective the Cold War was an interruption and the end of the Cold War stressed the necessity to get eyes back on the ball.

What is the writing on that ball? It is that martial conflict is ineradicable but not irreducible, and that economic conflict is no less dangerous or even lethal but the defences against it are much flimsier. There is a widespread perception of the horrors and stupidity of war, even among those who resort to it, but these is no such widespread perception of the perils and imminence of economic conflict; and the Cold War, with its emphasis on military pacts and nuclear war, made economic war seem relatively harmless. Mechanisms for obviating martial conflicts exist even though they have failed to come up to expectations; mechanisms for handling economic conflicts are much more embryonic. Yet the world's producers are failing, either in the volume of their production or in its distribution, to satisfy the elementary economic needs of the world's consumers and these consumers, multiplying at an unprecedented pace, can neither be fed where they are nor migrate freely to countries where they might be fed. Pressures to maintain or improve existing standards of life produce economic chauvinism and protectionism, beggar-my-neighbour clashes, which international organisations fail to resolve. These conflicts are becoming the most intractable form of the tussle between particularism and universalism, between parts and whole, in a world where a part, however powerful, can no longer conduct itself as though it were a whole.

All associations of unequal partners require an accommodation between the equal rights of the partners and the recognition of their unequal weight. In the United Nations this problem is met by giving some members a permanent seat in the Security Council with a veto. One aim of this arrangement is to vest leadership where power is and to counter the diffusion of responsibility among many members by focusing it on a select few – with the corollary that bodies like the Security Council may be destroyed if their leading members stint or subvert them. In the governing bodies of the World Bank and the International Monetary Fund similar provisions on membership and weighted voting rule. In the economic sphere an alternative pattern was tried with the creation in the 1980s of a distinct body restricted to the world's few most powerful economic states. This was the Group of Five finance ministers of the United States, Japan, Germany, France and Britain which was established in 1982 and became four years later the Group of Seven (G7) by the addition, for political rather than economic reasons, of Italy and Canada. The strength of the group was its smallness; its weakness the doubt whether it was a forum for compromises or for constructive propulsion. In the 1980s its positive impact came from the close Franco-German partnership exemplified by Valerie Giscard d'Estaing and Helmut Schmidt who, besides pioneering a European Monetary System, sought through the Plaza and Louvre Accords to devise ways for the orderly control of currencies used worldwide after the evaporation of Bretton Woods. But after this spurt of leadership the G7 lapsed into *ad hoc* tinkering, sidestepping the strains caused by a grossly overvalued yen and huge Japanese trade surpluses, by the damage done to the dollar through indisciplined budgeting, and by acrimonious stalemate in the Uruguay Round of the General Agreement on Tariffs and Trade (GATT) talks. It failed also to confront realistically the consequences of the end of the Cold War and, particularly, hyperinflation in Russia with its attendant political dangers.

The world's most pressing needs as the century approaches its end include therefore greater ingenuity in devising mechanisms to handle economic crises and current international economic affairs. No less pressing is the need to review the legal competence and practical capacity of the Security Council in the handling of political conflict and crises. The founding members of the United Nations envisaged the use of force under the aegis of the Security Council to keep the peace in certain circumstances and within certain limitations, but there are in the Charter ambiguities and inconsistencies and there have been since the signing of the Charter considerable changes in the perceived causes of the ills which the Security Council is to prevent or remedy. A series of calamities has emphasised the need to resolve these ambiguities one way or another in order to facilitate timely and effective action, while the very multiplication of these calamities – Bosnia receives most attention but is neither more horrible nor more dangerous than Angola, Somalia, Liberia, Cambodia – has demonstrated the need to limit the ambit of international intervention to what is practicable and what is seen by governments and peoples to be practicable. Such an assessment would also come clean about what in the present state of the world cannot be undertaken and ought therefore not to be supposed to be possible. These questions are being discussed, but randomly; they need to be addressed by small (or, to begin with, very small) groups of people whose views, commanding attention by their good sense rather than by the eminence of their originators, will gradually catch on until a set of proposals emerges fit to be presented to the secretary-general of the United Nations for debate by the Security Council. This is the opportunity created by the end of that unruly episode, the Cold War. But it is no mere opportunity. It is an imperative, for there is scarcely anything more frightening in the world today than the probable consequences of failing to define the practicalities of action and of the partnership between the United Nations and its most powerful members, particularly the United States of America.

INDEX

Note: some passing references omitted; footnotes denoted by f.

INDEX